Cambridge Elements

Elements in Ancient Philosophy
edited by
James Warren
University of Cambridge

ARISTIPPUS OF CYRENE, PLEASURE AND THE PRESENT

Georgia Mouroutsou
King's University College and Western University

Shaftesbury Road, Cambridge CB2 8EA, United Kingdom

One Liberty Plaza, 20th Floor, New York, NY 10006, USA

477 Williamstown Road, Port Melbourne, VIC 3207, Australia

314–321, 3rd Floor, Plot 3, Splendor Forum, Jasola District Centre, New Delhi – 110025, India

103 Penang Road, #05–06/07, Visioncrest Commercial, Singapore 238467

Cambridge University Press is part of Cambridge University Press & Assessment, a department of the University of Cambridge.

We share the University's mission to contribute to society through the pursuit of education, learning and research at the highest international levels of excellence.

www.cambridge.org
Information on this title: www.cambridge.org/9781009766708

DOI: 10.1017/9781009766661

© Georgia Mouroutsou 2025

This publication is in copyright. Subject to statutory exception and to the provisions of relevant collective licensing agreements, no reproduction of any part may take place without the written permission of Cambridge University Press & Assessment.

When citing this work, please include a reference to the DOI 10.1017/9781009766661

First published 2025

A catalogue record for this publication is available from the British Library

ISBN 978-1-009-76670-8 Hardback
ISBN 978-1-009-76669-2 Paperback
ISSN 2631-4118 (online)
ISSN 2631-410X (print)

Cambridge University Press & Assessment has no responsibility for the persistence or accuracy of URLs for external or third-party internet websites referred to in this publication and does not guarantee that any content on such websites is, or will remain, accurate or appropriate.

For EU product safety concerns, contact us at Calle de José Abascal, 56, 1°, 28003 Madrid, Spain, or email eugpsr@cambridge.org

Aristippus of Cyrene, Pleasure and the Present

Elements in Ancient Philosophy

DOI: 10.1017/9781009766661
First published online: December 2025

Georgia Mouroutsou
King's University College and Western University

Author for correspondence: Georgia Mouroutsou, gmourout@uwo.ca

Abstract: This Element offers a new historical account of Aristippus the Elder's views on pleasure and the present. Instead of treating Aristippus as merely proto-Cyrenaic or anachronistically modern, it uncovers in the ancient sources a neglected form of hedonism that endorses a present-focused therapeutic policy, while exploring its underlying motivations. Aristippan hedonism promotes a moment-to-moment disposition to pleasure rather than its maximization through future calculation, supporting a euthymic model of well-being that prioritizes the present. After distinguishing Aristippus from the later Cyrenaics regarding hedonic calculations to maximize pleasure, the Element yet supports continuity with his followers in the cognitive elements of the concept and the experience of pleasure, challenging his alleged sensualism in this way. Once the historical groundwork is in place, the Element introduces the hypothesis of the plasticity of the present, which moves beyond historical interpretation to offer an ethical-psychological account of a sustained focus on present time.

Keywords: ancient philosophy, Aristippus of Cyrene, Pleasure, Prudential Hedonism, Presentism

© Georgia Mouroutsou 2025

ISBNs: 9781009766708 (HB), 9781009766692 (PB), 9781009766661 (OC)
ISSNs: 2631-4118 (online), 2631-410X (print)

Contents

1 Introducing Aristippus of Cyrene: Challenges and Objectives   1

2 A Historical Reconstruction   5

3 Beyond Historical Reconstruction: Aristippus and the 'Plasticity of the Present'   59

    List of Abbreviations   64

    References   67

1 Introducing Aristippus of Cyrene: Challenges and Objectives

Aristippus, born in the Greek colony of Cyrene in ancient Libya, moved to Athens, drawn by tales of Socrates. Plutarch reports he became so infatuated upon meeting Socrates that he literally fell ill – a reaction reflecting a complex experience of pleasure and pain, both intellectual and bodily, verging on erotic pangs:

> When Aristippus met Ischomachus at Olympia, he asked him with what kind of conversation Socrates was disposed toward the young people. When he received a few tiny seeds and samples of Socrates' words, he was so affected that he broke down physically and became completely pale and feeble until, after having sailed to Athens, he drew water from the fountain with burning thirst. He studied the man and his words and his philosophy that aims at getting to know one's ills and getting rid of them.
>
> Plut. *De Cur.* 516C2–10 / *SSR* IV A 2[1]

Aristippus was the most provocative companion of Socrates in that he boldly endorsed pleasure as a central value – an attitude that brought him fame, or rather infamy. Xenophon, another contemporary and follower of Socrates, presents Aristippus critically as someone lacking control over bodily desires in a dialogue where Socrates tries to convince him of the importance of self-discipline (*Mem.* II.1). Likewise, Xenophon disapproves of Aristippus' refusal to engage in political life. Plato, too, mentions Aristippus disparagingly – criticizing his apparent disloyalty for not visiting Socrates in prison, despite being nearby in Aegina (*Phaedo* 59 c).

Yet, Aristippus is also reported to have practised Socratic elenchus (*Mem.* III.8)[2] and to have written dialogues on topics such as wisdom and education, as noted in two lists preserved by Diogenes Laertius (II.83–85). Although none of his works survive, Aristippus clearly belongs to Socrates' circle. He exemplifies the Socratic commitment to dialogue and virtue – while uniquely emphasizing the cultivation of pleasure through trained self-control, rather than its suppression (see *Sent. Vat.* 34; *SSR* IV A 124).

Aristippus is generally seen as a fourth-century BCE hedonist, who presented his philosophy in a notably unsystematic way through pithy remarks and a provocative lifestyle. While his role as founder of the Cyrenaic School is

---

[1] Unless otherwise indicated, translations are mine. See Lampe 2015, 204f. on the reliability of the anecdotal tradition. For my purposes – namely, to reconstruct Aristippus' beliefs philosophically – I agree with Tsouna-McKirahan 1994, 387–91, that the anecdotes reveal the ancient conception of philosophy as a way of life, and thus present it in action. I am not concerned with the anecdotes' historical veracity, on which see Kindstrand 1986 and Goldhill 2009.

[2] Tsouna 2020, 391, highlights Aristippus' collaborative spirit and desire to learn, balancing Xenophon's negative portrait and critique.

attested, it remains disputed.³ Although he did not elaborate his positions theoretically, he was taken seriously as an interlocutor and opponent. The existence of works bearing his name suggests his views warranted attention. Speusippus, Plato's successor and an anti-hedonist, wrote a treatise titled *Aristippus*.⁴ Aristotle criticizes Aristippus' dismissal of mathematics as irrelevant to ethics. In *Met.* II.996a18–996b2, he links this view to sophists who deny the ethical value of mathematics. He responds in *Met.* XII.1078a31–1078b7, addressing the role of final causes in mathematical inquiry, again alluding to this group without naming Aristippus. According to Philodemus, Epicurus read Aristippus' writings on Plato, attesting to his ongoing relevance in ancient philosophical debates.⁵

Clement of Alexandria presents an ambiguous view of Aristippus. In one passage, he links Aristippus' attitude to pleasure with sophistic arrogance. After mentioning an unnamed heretic who claimed to conquer pleasure by indulging in it, Clement introduces Aristippus as similarly deceived by hedonistic fallacies (*Strom.* II.20.117–118; *SSR* IV A 96). Elsewhere, discussing the proper use of ointments, Clement contrasts sensual arousal with healing utility and refers to Aristippus as a philosopher who lived luxuriously and defended the healing value of ointments, criticizing the catamites who rejected them (*Paedag.* II.8.64; *SSR* IV A 64).

Aristippus the Elder favoured hedonism in both lifestyle and views; Carneades, the leading head of the Sceptical Academy, even made him hedonism's chief representative, in preference to Epicurus (Cic. *Fin.* 5.7–20; *SSR* IV A 187). Nonetheless, the Cyrenaic system of hedonism was quickly eclipsed by the more refined version of hedonism that Epicurus offered in the Hellenistic period. Epicurus' success stemmed partly from addressing Cyrenaic challenges, offered by later Cyrenaic sects, and partly from offering a more consistent and sophisticated hedonistic ethics.⁶

Despite the Cyrenaics' early eclipse, polemical engagement between Epicurean and Cyrenaic views persisted in later testimonies, both hostile and sympathetic to the Cyrenaics: Cicero, an Academic Sceptic, Plutarch, a middle-Platonist, and Sextus Empiricus, a Pyrrhonian Sceptic, are sympathetic; Philodemus (late Hellenistic) and Diogenes of Oinoanda (Imperial period),

---

[3] See Tsouna-McKirahan 1994 on Hellenistic historiography influencing the continuous succession of ancient schools and debates on Aristippus' role as Cyrenaic founder; also Mannebach 1961, 86–93.

[4] For whether Speusippus targeted Aristippus directly or as a proxy for Eudoxus, see Döring 1988, 67, and Tarán 1981, 191–2.

[5] See *SSR* IV A 147, that is, Epicurus fragment 118 Arrighetti¹, 127 Arrhighetti².

[6] See Long 1999 and Tsouna 2016 on Cyrenaic–Epicurean interrelations, the latter expanding on Long's brief formulation.

both Epicureans, and Aristocles, an Aristotelian of the early Roman Imperial period, are unsympathetic.

Against this historical background, reconstructing Aristippus' own views is an ambitious – perhaps impossible – task. We lack primary texts, and extant testimonies are sparse and often confounded by his grandson, Aristippus the Younger, who articulated Cyrenaic thought more clearly (see Aristocles' later testimony), inspired by his grandfather and taught by his mother. These conditions invite arguments *ex silentio* and the projection of various assumptions onto a fundamentally indeterminate corpus. Moreover, our sources often deploy Cyrenaics polemically – either to discredit them (Epicureans, Platonists, Aristotelians, Christians) or to discredit Epicureans through them (as in academic writers like Cicero and Plutarch). When Aristippus is associated with seizing the day (*carpe diem*), it is often understood as short-term indulgence in present vulgar pleasures motivated by an irrational fear of death.[7]

Even the idea that Aristippus' thought contains anything philosophical has been challenged. His views appear to be pre-philosophical at best.[8] A question about the theoretical conception of a philosophical life that fits Aristippus – who shows no interest in theoretical explanation – is predisposed to yield a negative answer, suggesting he simply lives without explaining.[9] The first step away from this impasse is to change the question. This Element instead asks which philosophical theories and concepts best do justice to Aristippus, honouring the spirit of the sources even when going beyond them.

Beyond this core challenge lies a long-standing debate over the Cyrenaics' and Aristippus' stance on eudaemonism – the view that the ultimate goal of human action is flourishing extending throughout the entire life. Their focus on present pleasures has led some scholars to see them as rejecting this prevailing framework of ancient Greek ethics.[10] On this score, extant reports on Aristippus seem to conflict: some appear to show disregard for the future, others align more with care about it. My interpretation (Section 2.2) offers a distinctive

---

[7] See Phld. *De elect*. XVII; with Indelli and Tsouna-McKirahan 1995, 195–200) on Aristippus' anti-rationalist escape from death; and Athenaeus' view of present-focus as profligate – a view I later challenge by exploring alternative motivations for Aristippus' hedonism.

[8] In this spirit, Tsouna 2020 denies hedonism as attributable to him. Section 2.1 argues for his hedonism.

[9] Mann 1996, 119: 'There is nothing to Aristippus' philosophy, besides the way he lives his life. That life is not to be explained, but shown. That life is not to be given a positive justification. Yet one might come to see its appeal.' Though I do not share his extreme conclusion, I separate Aristippus from later Cyrenaics, too, to avoid anachronistic projection.

[10] Irwin 1991 began the debate by reconstructing an Aristippan anti-eudaemonism based on the rejection of a continuous self by blurring the line between historical interpretation and philosophical reconstruction; for critical reaction see Tsouna 1998, 132–3 and 2002, and O'Keefe 2002, 398–401. Annas 1993 defends Aristippus' anti-eudaemonism.

contribution by showing how Aristippus' focus on the present is compatible with future concern and a whole-life perspective while setting his thought apart from later considerations of the hedonic calculus and from 'presentism' as couched in contemporary metaphysics and ethics.[11]

Another less developed topic is the role of cognition in the experience of pleasure.[12] Sections 2.3–4 challenge the common assumption that Aristippus regarded pleasure as merely sensory and will argue that, for Aristippus as for later Cyrenaics, pleasure is fundamentally attitudinal and cognitively informed. While Section 2.2 distinguishes Aristippus' approach from the later hedonic calculus, Sections 2.3–4 explore a continuity in the cognitive dimension of pleasure, with Aristippus as a link between Plato's *Philebus* and Hellenistic successors. As a Socratic and contemporary of Plato, Aristippus is likely to reflect discussions in Plato's circle. By saying he 'reflects' these discussions, I do not claim that Aristippus adopts or originates Plato's account in the *Philebus*, but rather that he occupies a distinct role within the Cyrenaic School, mediating and transmitting certain ideas to later Cyrenaics.

This Element uncovers in the ancient sources a neglected form of hedonism that endorses a present-focused therapeutic policy, and, inspired by Plato's educational dialectic with hedonists such as Protagoras (and the fictive masses) and Callicles,[13] explores its underlying motivations. Aristippan hedonism promotes a moment-to-moment attitude to pleasure rather than its maximization through future calculation, articulating a eudaemonistic approach centred on the present. While distinguishing Aristippus from later Cyrenaics[14] on the question of hedonic calculation, the study also highlights continuities in the cognitive elements of pleasure – challenging the common portrayal of Aristippus as a sensualist[15] – as well as in their therapeutic strategies.

---

[11] Both O'Keefe 2002 and Warren 2014a examine why the Cyrenaics – not specifically Aristippus – focused on the present, contrasting with Epicurean eudaemonism. O'Keefe reconstructs their emphasis on present, shifting desires, rooted in epistemological subjectivism. Warren connects current debates on time-relativity (the present has special importance over past and future) and time-neutrality (the present has no special importance) to Cyrenaic–Epicurean contrasts, explaining the Cyrenaic focus as stemming from pessimism about effectively applying prudential reasoning via the hedonic calculus (Warren 2001, 165f.), thus expanding what Gosling and Taylor 1982, 42, had briefly suggested. There is no textual evidence for present *desires* nor pessimism in Aristippus.
[12] Warren 2013 has devoted a separate study to this topic and the differences between the Epicureans and the Cyrenaics on the *pathos* of pleasure; my approach builds on his by focusing specifically on Aristippus' contribution.
[13] I develop this in detail in my *Therapeutic Dialectic: Plato and the Hedonists in the Protagoras and the Gorgias* (manuscript nearing completion).
[14] See Rowe 2015 on what separates and connects Aristippus and the later Cyrenaics.
[15] Feldman 2006, 30–4.

2 A Historical Reconstruction
2.1 Which *Telos*? Which Hedonism?

This section defends the claim that Aristippus was an ethical hedonist and that, if and when he used the word *telos* – certainly without systematizing it – he probably operated with a 'twofold *telos*', understanding *telos* in the sense of 'outcome': pleasure is the outcome of good things, pain of bad. The 'twofold *telos*' emerges succinctly in pseudo-Plutarch's *Strom.* 9: 'Aristippus of Cyrene says that the end of the good things is pleasure and the end of the bad things is pain (*telos agathōn tēn hēdonēn, kakōn de algēdona*).'[16] One should, of course, proceed with caution regarding the truth of what is attested in *Stromateis*. I begin with it because it offers a complete and succinct report of a view attributed to the older Aristippus. The alternative meaning of *telos* as 'that for the sake of which',[17] was made part of formal philosophical terminology by Aristotle. Before that decisive turn, its earlier meaning was 'what something ends in': the end of a time period, one's life (i.e., death), or a process (i.e., the resulting state). A broad range of literature, including Homer, Herodotus, and the tragic poets, attests to this earlier usage.[18] Plato develops the twofold *telos* (as good or bad outcome) in *Prot.* 352c1–355a5, applying the usual sense of 'what something results in' to frame a hedonistic consequentialism: for the hedonists Socrates engages with and improves, what is good ends in future pleasure, what is bad in future pain – regardless of present experience, which may be the opposite (e.g., a painful treatment ending in health's pleasure, or pleasant adultery ending in a divorce). Aristippus – as we shall see – rejects *this kind* of future orientation. That Plato here draws on a contemporary while modifying and, in his view, improving the idea is plausible and unsurprising: writing as an educating philosopher, not a mere doxographer, he actively corrects others, including going against their spirit when he sees fit.

Aristippus most likely used *telos* in its 'everyday sense' and understood present pleasure as the good outcome. It would be remarkable if he adopted the later Aristotelian sense, despite two scattered appearances in Plato

---

[16] *SSR* IV A 166 / Mannebach 144 (*Dox. Graec.* p. 581.22).
[17] I do not count Lampe's translation of *telos* – 'the fullest, highest, most complete expression of the following adjective' – as a serious alternative. Though contextually tailored, it awkwardly merges 'highest goal' with semantics and, needless to add, is anachronistic and far too refined to suit Aristippus.
[18] Allen 2014 traces the semantic history of *telos* to explain the notion of the outcome of bad things in Cicero's *De finibus bonorum et malorum*, rescuing Cicero from interpretations that claim he erred in the title by implying that bad things could be aimed at if conceived as such. The outcome of good and bad things in Cicero and elsewhere would not puzzle someone familiar with modern Greek, where both meanings survive: although Aristotle's sense became dominant in philosophy, the earlier, more familiar one has persisted for millennia.

(*Gorg.* 499e; *Tim.* 90d). That Aristippus reproached Plato for being too professorial (*epaggeltikōteron ti eiponta*), unlike Socrates (Arist. *Rh.* 1398b31–4), suggests he preferred common usage over new philosophical terminology.[19] Nevertheless, complications arise because later sources often use the Aristotelian sense of *telos* – as final cause or that-for-the-sake-of-which – alongside the older meaning, even when discussing Aristippus.

Now let us return to pseudo-Plutarch's *Stromateis* 9 quoted above. The author ascribes to Aristippus a 'twofold end': the end of good things is pleasure and the end of bad things is pain, with *telos* necessarily meaning what these things result in; for the only other alternative for the construction *telos kakōn* would be self-contradictory; for one does not aim at a bad thing, let alone rank evils in a hierarchy of goals.[20] After attributing the twofold end to him, the author reports that Aristippus endorsed ethics as the only worthwhile inquiry, a view confirmed in multiple sources: Eus. *PE* XV.62.7 (*SSR* IVA 166; Mannebach 145) attributes that stance to Aristippus and the Stoic Aristo; Themistius (*Or.* 34.5) includes Aristippus among Socrates' followers who privileged ethics; Seneca (*Ep.* 89) criticizes the Cyrenaics for rejecting physics and logic while still addressing them in ethics; Sextus Empiricus (*M.* VII.11) confirms this view critically (*SSR* IV A 168; Mannebach 147A, 148).

Our cautious conclusion therefore is that when Aristippus used *telos*, it was in the sense of 'outcome' – not as goal – since pain, one of the two *telē*, is no goal.

Aristocles of Messene, an Aristotelian philosopher of the first century CE, provides valuable insight into Aristippus in his work *On Philosophy*, parts of which are preserved in Eusebius (*PE*). Unlike other sources, Aristocles does not degrade him as a profligate. We will examine the relevant passage, fragment F5 in Chiesara's edition, to show that it portrays Aristippus as someone who valued pleasure as *the* good.[21] Fragment F5 comes from Eusebius' introduction to the Aristotelian's work, not from Aristocles who is directly quoted later.

Aristocles criticizes the Cyrenaic view that only affections are *katalēpta* (apprehensible). Eusebius, in his introductions to Aristocles, traces Epicurus' *On the End* (*telos*) back to Aristippus, who initiated the hedonist line.[22] Eusebius does not clarify the sense of *telos*, likely because he uses it in the

---

[19] Mann 1996, 117f., reads *epaggeltikōteron eipein* as rash dogmatism and takes Aristippus' avoidance as naïve scepticism – an anachronistic imposition unsupported by any evidence here or elsewhere.

[20] The appropriate Greek for *summum malorum* would have been *to megiston kakōn*, not *telos kakōn*.

[21] *Pace* Tsouna 2020, it will be shown that Aristocles does not oppose the mainstream tradition depicting the Socratic as a hedonist.

[22] Aristocles F8, critical of Epicurean hedonism, claims that the Epicureans' starting point was the Aristippan way of life (*diagōgē*).

common philosophical sense of 'goal' and not 'end result'. Nevertheless, the passage is especially valuable for its insights into Aristippus' lifestyle and terminology for pleasure:

> One would make counterarguments akin to those [i.e., the preceding arguments against the Pyrrhonian Sceptics that nothing is apprehensible, F4] to the followers of Aristippus of Cyrene, who say that only affections are apprehensible. Aristippus was a friend of Socrates, and was the founder of the sect that is called Cyrenaic. With regard to the way of life, Aristippus was very soft and fond of pleasure; that said, [a] he did not openly engage in dialectic at all about the end (*ouden men houtos en tō phanerōi peri telous dielexato*) [b] but implicitly kept on saying that the substance of happiness lies in pleasures (*dynamei de tēs eudaimonias tēn hypostasin elegen en hēdonais keisthai*) since by perpetually making pleasure the subject of his discourses (*aei gar logous peri hēdonēs poioumenos*), he led those who were present with him to apprehend him to say that living pleasantly is the end.[23]

That Aristippus is described as *philēdonos* confirms that *telos* here means 'goal' – he loves or desires (*philein*) pleasures. His not publicly discussing the *telos* suggests not that he lacked views on the matter, but that he did not formulate or share a systematic *telos*-theory like Epicurus. But this omission does not challenge the attribution to him of ethical hedonism. Aristippus implies that happiness lies *en hēdonais* – in pleasures. We must unpack what this claim asserts, what it does not, and clarify its contrast in the *men–de* clause, marked as [a] and [b] in the translation above.

The opposition is between [a] speaking openly about the *telos*, and [b] implying that pleasures are where happiness lies. Crucially, Eusebius uses the plural *en hēdonais*, suggesting that Aristippus implied happiness lies in the plurality of – many particular – pleasures, not in a general notion of pleasure. Perhaps the philosopher hesitated to claim publicly happiness lies in pleasures, though this seems inconsistent with his character traits and behaviours as manifest in the anecdotological material.[24]

Even so, the statement remains vague: how exactly do particular pleasures constitute happiness?[25] Eusebius does not clarify, likely because Aristippus did not either. What is clear is that Aristippus treats pleasure – not in the abstract,

---

[23] *SSR* IV A 173 / Mannebach 126C, 80 and 155.
[24] A contrast between the conception of pleasure as a final cause (*telos*) and as a material cause – the concrete constituents (*hēdonai*, in the plural) of a good life – is less probable, as it would attribute to Aristippus an interest in a kind of causal theory with which he does not engage explicitly. However, Aristocles may have reconstructed his thought as implicitly framing pleasures as material causes.
[25] When Diogenes Laertius focuses on Aristippus' followers, he speaks of happiness as the accumulation (*athroismos*) or the sum total (*systēma*) of pleasures (D.L. II.89 and 87 respectively) without suggesting the way of calculating the particular pleasures.

but *pleasures* in the plural – as the only good. Had Eusebius or his source intended to say that Aristippus valued pleasure as one good among others, it would have been easy to say so – but no such indication appears.

Aristippus is reported to have talked about pleasure constantly with his companions. Unlike the eponymous character in Plato's *Philebus*, he was not content with private indulgence but actively discussed pleasure. By giving pleasure – or rather, *pleasures* – pride of place, Aristippus led others to infer that for him *to hēdeōs zēn* is the *telos*.[26] We must take this as his view: living pleasantly constitutes the good life.[27] Eusebius next turns to Aristippus the Younger, the Elder's grandson, who clearly (*saphōs*) defined *to hēdeōs zēn* as the *telos*, unlike his grandfather who did so only implicitly (*dunamei*). Contrary to his grandfather, the younger Cyrenaic treated particular pleasures as final causes.[28]

An additional source attributes 'the twofold outcome' to the Cyrenaics generally, not to Aristippus the Elder in particular: Sextus Empiricus, *M.* VII.199–200 (*SSR* IV A 213 / Mannebach 167). Having argued for the twofold-end view in Aristippus, we now draw on this Sceptic philosopher to complete the set of sources referring to such a theory. In a discussion of dogmatic criteria of truth, Sextus reports that the Cyrenaics recognized three types of affection: pleasant, painful, and neutral:

> For the affections extend over [the realm of] ends; for some of the affections are pleasant, some are painful and some are in-between. And the painful ones are, they say, evils, whose outcome is pain, the pleasant ones are goods, whose outcome is pleasure without mistake, and the intermediates are neither good nor bad, whose outcome is the neither-good-nor-evil, this being an affection between pleasure and pain.

The source recognizes pleasure and pain as two outcomes, the neutral affections being added to those. In all three cases, the meaning of *telos* is what the affections end in. Sextus states the three affections with their respective *telos*,

---

[26] The present infinitive ('living pleasantly') could refer to either a whole (present) pleasant life or the present pleasures.

[27] Beyond a mere description of his life, it could also be read as a suggestion about how one should live. I do not share the certainty with which Tsouna 2020, 384, denies its normative character.

[28] Mann 1996, 116–7, argues that since *telos* as 'goal' was unavailable to Aristippus, his hedonism must be non-dogmatic and impressionistic. In the discussion on 14 April 2024, Andrea Falcon raised a similar concern: how can one affirm hedonism without treating pleasure as a final cause? Yet it is unclear why pleasure cannot be *the* good without Aristotelian causal theory. After all, and though the terminology was not yet fixed, our ancient sources regularly attribute views on the *telos* to pre-Platonic and pre-Aristotelian figures. Greek offered many ways – beyond *telos* – to express what one values or pursues. Aristippus' frequent focus on pleasure supports his hedonism: it was the only thing he consistently valued.

and what they end in.²⁹ I understand the crucial relative clauses (*hōn telos algēdōn / hōn telos estin adiapseuston hēdonē / hōn telos to oute agathon oute kakon*) as non-restrictive,³⁰ for restrictive sentences would make no sense: what would the evils end in other than pain, and what would the goods end in other than pleasure according to hedonists? Even differently inclined hedonists who would align with consequentialism as described in the discussion of hedonism in Plato's *Protagoras* would not agree: there are things that are painful at present but pay off in future pleasure; because of that future pleasure, they call them good and not bad. Moreover, a completion of the categorization would be expected in the passage in the case that we had bad, painful things that do not end in pain.³¹

We have argued that Aristippus of Cyrene was committed to ethical hedonism (pleasures are the only goods) but that it is very plausible that when using the word *telos*, he understood it as what something ends in (the outcome of good things, that is, present pleasant things, being present pleasure, and the outcome of bad things, that is, present painful things, being present pain, which will be analyzed in what follows) and not as the *summum bonum*. We have found a spurious piece of evidence of the twofold *telos* in pseudo-Plutarch and Sextus Empiricus making use of it without elaborating. Plato, instead, provides us with the longest extant explanation of a two-*telos* hedonistic theory based on the original meaning of *telos* in the *Protagoras*, and in particular, 353c1–355a5, which was possibly inspired by this Aristippan outlook.

2.2 Aristippus as a 'Paronist'

2.2.1 The Evidence from Athenaeus

In this section, we further elaborate how Aristippus understood the nature of pleasures: how he discerned their value and how he described the proper attitude toward both pleasure and pain. For this, I draw from Athenaeus of Naucratis, a contemporary of Marcus Aurelius. Alongside Aelian – who outlived Athenaeus – these sources will help define Aristippan *paronism*, a neologism coined here

---

[29] *Telos* appears only five more times in *M.* VII / *M.* XI, meaning 'goal': VII.158.4 (*eudaimonia* as life's *telos*); XI.106.1 (sceptical *telos*); XI.144.5; XI.167.2; XI.179.5 (Epicurus: *telos* of *eudaimonia* is pleasure).

[30] I agree about this with Bury 1935, Bett 2005, and Allen 2014.

[31] Tsouna 1998, 156, omits a comma after *evils*, likely a typo ('and the painful ones are, they say, evils whose end is pain, the pleasant ones are goods, whose unmistakeable end is pleasure'). Thus, it is unclear how she understands the relative clauses – restrictively or non-restrictively – since it would be odd to interpret one as restrictive and the other as non-restrictive, and not clear as in Allen 2014, 236.

based on the Greek *to paron* ('the present') (2.2.1–3).³² I present the two important passages below with numbered divisions for ease of reference, as I will compare parts of the testimonies.

Text A (Athenaeus)

(1) And entire schools of philosophers laid claim to the choice of luxury; for example, the one they call the Cyrenaic School, which originated with Aristippus the Socratic. Having endorsed *being affected by pleasant things* [*hēdupatheia*] he said that *this is the end*, and that happiness is based on it.

(2) And he said that it [being affected by pleasant things] is of a single time [*monochronon*], and thinking, more or less as profligates do, that neither the memory of past enjoyments nor the hope for future ones were anything in relation to him, but *judging the good by the one and only criterion of the present.* He held that having enjoyed, and enjoying in the future is nothing in relation to him because the first is no longer and the second is not yet and is uncertain; which is the sort of thing that happens to the indulgent, who raise the claim to fare well regarding the present.

Athen. *Deipnosophistae* XII.544 A–B.³³

Text B (Aelian)

(1) Aristippus had seemed to speak in an exceedingly rigorous manner, exhorting people *not to toil afterwards over what has passed or strain themselves in advance about what is coming*; (2) *for, such an attitude is a sign of cheerfulness and a proof of a gracious mind.*

(3) He prescribed that people keep their thought *on the day*, and again on that part within the day in which each one takes some action or thinks; *for only the present is ours*, he said, *not what has gone by or what is anticipated, for the one is lost, and the other is uncertain if indeed it will be.*

Gel. *VH* XIV.6³⁴

The language of Text A (1) displays a degree of openness and vagueness characteristic of Aristippus' unsystematic views. While elements of later Cyrenaic doctrine may also be conflated in the text, a helpful criterion for us to use is whether Aristippus could have used such language non-systematically

---

³² I avoid the term 'presentism', introduced by Graver 2002 and adopted by Lampe 2015, to steer clear of the unwanted connotations and allusions to modern ontological theories of time and some modern ethical debates.

³³ *SSR* IV A 174 / Mannebach 207.

³⁴ This is the second part of *SSR* IV A 174 / Mannebach 208.

or anachronistically – whether, for example, he could have thought of the present as described, without developing a theory. The strategy, then, is to reduce the views to something he could plausibly have held and for which we have some external support.

My translation emphasizes what the compound *hēdupatheia* conveys: pleasure as being affected (*paschein*) by pleasant things (*hupo tōn hēdeōn*).[35] This choice is more appropriate than the simpler 'pleasure' (*hēdonē*) which is ambiguous, potentially referring either to the state of being pleased or to the pleasant object causing the affection (*to hēdesthai* or *to hēdu*, respectively). The Aristippan point reported here is that the *telos* lies in the internal, subjective experience of being pleased – not in the external pleasant object.

That pleasure is a specific kind of affection (*pathos*) is already attested for the father of the Cyrenaics in the definition of *telos* found in Diogenes Laertius. Diogenes' report is striking, as it is the only philosophical claim that he attributes to Aristippus after a long series of anecdotes about his life and a list of works he is said to have written. For this reason, we must carefully assess what it reveals about pleasure as both *pathos* and *telos*:

> *Telos d' apephaine tēn leian kinēsin eis aisthēsin anadidomenēn.*
> He asserted that the 'end' is the smooth motion that is distributed to perception. D.L. II.85

We are presented with an unqualified assertion about the *telos*, clearly attributed to Aristippus. This is significant: it is the final line assigned to him before Diogenes Laertius turns to later Cyrenaics. The clear definition of pleasure in the sentence allows *telos* to take on either of two meanings – either as the object of all desire (akin to the final cause in Aristotelian or post-Aristotelian contexts), or as the end-result of all good things, that is, of pleasant things.

Three key points emerge about the nature of pleasure:

1. Pleasure as a kind of motion: Pleasure is described as a *smooth motion*, a view adopted by later Cyrenaics as well, in contrast to pain, which they characterize as *harsh motion*. The affective experience (*pathos*) of being pleased results from a unique, unrepeatable interaction between the perceiver and a pleasant object under specific conditions. Later Cyrenaic epistemology supports this account.
2. Motion and perception: That this smooth motion is 'distributed to perception' implies that not every motion produces perception – an idea familiar

---

[35] 'Living pleasantly' (Lampe 2015) is ambiguous regarding whether it refers to the entire life or the present pleasure; 'this life of easy-going pleasure' (Gulick 1933) is acceptable but misses the nuance; 'every pleasurable passion' (Tsouna 2020) is better, but I avoid it as particularity is not yet introduced in the text.

from Plato's *Philebus*. Only perceived restorative motions are pleasant, whereas many bodily motions go unnoticed and are therefore affectively neutral.
3. Inclusion of all pleasures: The statement applies to all pleasures, not just bodily or intellectual pleasures, nor exclusively to those of body or soul. Crucially, this is the only explicit philosophical view attributed to Aristippus by Diogenes, and it does not prioritize bodily pleasures over intellectual ones – a prioritization commonly (and wrongly) presumed and more justly associated with later Cyrenaics. This short report gives no such indication. What it confirms instead is the shared Cyrenaic principle that all pleasure is perceived.

An exclusive concern with bodily pleasures could plausibly motivate the primacy of present pleasures: bodily sensations are tied to the immediacy and intensity of the present moment. The body anchors experience in what is currently felt. On its own, it cannot transcend the immediacy of perception. By contrast, Epicureanism prioritizes intellectual over bodily pleasures and does not give primacy to the present moment, the mind's strength lying in its ability to traverse time, integrating past, present, and future. But Aristippus does not elevate bodily pleasures as the primary hedonic experiences, nor are they presented as merely sensual. He also acknowledges and enjoys intellectual pleasures. Therefore, the assumption that he must have given primacy to the present *because* he privileged bodily pleasures cannot be supported by the available sources.

The first two points – pleasure as perceived motion – echo a crucial and distinctive feature of Plato's analysis in the *Philebus*. Although *Philebus* doesn't offer an explicit definition of pleasure, it employs a working notion of pleasure as *plērōsis tēs endeias*, a 'filling of a lack' for all pleasures, both bodily and intellectual. Thus, the third point too – the inclusion of all pleasures, though not understood as restorative by the Cyrenaic – finds resonance.

While we cannot definitively show whether Aristippus influenced or originated any elements in Plato's account of pleasure, the reverse idea – that Aristippus reflects discussions circulating in Socratic and Platonic circles – is far more plausible than the alternative possibility that he mirrors later Hellenistic developments. Those developments – such as Epicureanism or Sceptic advancements – presuppose theories that emerged only after Aristippus' time and would be anachronistic to read back into his thought.

By 'reflecting' contemporary discussions, I do not mean that Aristippus adopts or even anticipates Plato's analysis. Nor do I claim that he originated any part of it. Rather, I suggest that his distinctive contribution lies in his proximity to those intellectual conversations. Points 1 and 2 above, along with the cognitive aspects to be discussed in Section 2.3, support this interpretation of Aristippus' place and role in his school.

Having fleshed out the implications of the compound notion of *hēdupatheia* and connected the affection of pleasure to *telos* via Diogenes' testimony, we return to Athenaeus: What does it mean in A (1) that 'being pleased' is the *telos*? Here, *telos* most probably means 'that for the sake of which' (the later philosophical term). But Aristippus' meaning of 'what something ends in' can be accommodated too. The affection of being pleased is the final outcome – what all good things (which can only mean the pleasant things according to the hedonist) end in as what they cause – and at the same time, the most valuable goal one strives for. Eusebius had highlighted a plurality of pleasures (*hēdonai*), but with an ambiguity with regard to what pleasure refers to: the pleasant thing or the subjective feeling. *Hēdupatheia* clearly means the experience of pleasure. Though it is a singular noun, Athenaeus later introduces plurality with *apolauseis, to apolelaukenai,* and *to apolausein* – signalling multiple past and future moments of enjoyment. Thus, *hēdupatheia* plausibly refers to a plurality of particular pleasant experiences rather than a general state of being pleasantly affected. One might take each such experience to be unique and unrepeatable, without the underlying epistemology the later Cyrenaics offered: it is the plurality of pleasant experiences that constitutes the *telos*.

The idea that pleasant affectivity is the *telos* aligns with the bare minimum of (and nothing more than) Plato's *Protagoras*: it is the outcome that holds ultimate significance. For Aristippus, this priority holds its weight as the definitive and concluding moment. Athenaeus provides greater clarity than Eusebius by clarifying that *eudaimonia* is contingent on pleasure, not vice versa. The wording remains indeterminate, perhaps reflecting the Aristippan decision to refrain from entering philosophical terrain.[36] Though the nature of this dependency remains unclear, the notions of pleasure and *eudaimonia* are presented as distinct. A relevant question is whether and if so, in which respect, there is anything more to living a good life than living a life containing a plurality of pleasures[37] – and which pleasures, if any, have priority.

---

[36] The dependence is clear: the foundations of *eudaimonia* are said to be laid in pleasant affectivity – *en autēi tēn eudaimonian beblēsthai* (middle voice). Had Aristippus been more philosophically robust, *eudaimonia* would count as an *archē*, as the image implies. Ontological priority (Plato via Aristotle, *Metaph.* IV.11) lies beyond his horizon, and wouldn't be helpful to reconstruct his concerns: remove happiness, pleasures stay; remove pleasures, happiness collapses.

[37] A life of pleasures is not a life 'of as many pleasures as possible' but a life of training in pleasure, specifically in immersion and detachment, as will be shown – definitely a concern distinct from the pleasures.

Evidence from the later Cyrenaics clearly identifies specific pleasures – explicitly not *eudaimonia* – as the highest object of desire and value (*telos* as ultimate final cause).[38] Athenaeus, however, does not support this exclusion in reference to Aristippus. His report states that one steadily aims at the outcome of good (pleasant) things – namely, specific episodes of being pleased – which does not necessarily exclude *eudaimonia* as a goal. Since *eudaimonia* is grounded in pleasure, it remains desirable and worthy of concern. The message we might advance in A (1), avoiding reliance on the common slogan of unsystematicity, is that the text leaves open the possibility that both specific pleasures and *eudaimonia* are of concern. Given the focus on the present and the absence of any explicit statement identifying *eudaimonia* as a goal in the reports, it is reasonable to infer that *eudaimonia* is only an indirect or secondary concern.[39] In any case, the passage clearly rejects anti-*eudaimonism* as an Aristippan credo.

Certainly, Aristippus speaks *en dunamei* and leaves some precise points as yet underdetermined. For now, I have shown that the sources leave room to understand his thinking as accommodating overall happiness as a secondary focus and open space for a more nuanced reading of his concern for happiness. This opening is pivotal for developing the Aristippan 'therapeutic policy' in Section 2.2.3 in the spirit – rather than against the spirit – of the sources.

Given his concern with consequences, in particular the ultimate consequence (*telos*) of good things, Aristippus is principally a consequentialist. In another respect, he is not, for he does not represent the hedonism that Plato's Socrates portrays in the *Protagoras* that locates *telos* in the future or in the whole of a life, including time yet to be lived. The *telos* that Aristippus has in mind is rooted in the present: it is pleasure as the present and not the future outcome, caused by the present pleasant object, as is demonstrated in the immediate sequence of the report that introduces the crucial aspect of what is present: Text A (2).

Aristippus is reported as describing being pleased as *monochronos* – an unusual term. Its precise meaning, translation, and philosophical implications remain unclear. Semantically, Atheneaus – or his source – transfers a term from prosody to ethics to address pleasure's relation to time.[40] *LJS* defines *monochronos* as 'short-lived' or 'momentary', likely assuming an analogy with short (*monochrona*) versus long (*dichrona*) vowels. Yet this reading is problematic: it

---

[38] D.L. II.87–8; Clement of Alexandria, *Strom.* II.21.130.7–8.
[39] Athenaeus leaves two options open: either pleasure and *eudaimonia* based on pleasure coincide as the ultimate goal (as in Epicurus), or they are distinct yet related. Since *euthymia* as a disposition does not coincide with pleasure as an emotion, as we will see in Aelian's report, I already adopt the view of two distinct concerns in Aristippus.
[40] For *lexis* being *monochronos*, consider *Arc. De Acc.* 139.20; for *stoicheia*, *Sch. D. T.* 142 H.; for the opposite *dichronos*, Longin. *Proll. Heph.* 1.10, *Sch. D. T.* 127 H.

is counterintuitive to claim all pleasure is brief; think of pleasures like swimming or conversing with friends for a whole day.

Since metaphors need not carry all features from their original context, we should not transfer the notion of shortness from prosody. 'Momentary' misrepresents compounds with *mono-*, which denote singularity, not duration. Aristippus is not portrayed as being concerned with how long pleasure lasts or with ranking pleasures by duration. Nor does Athenaeus suggest that Aristippus linked pleasure to the present because it is fleeting. There is no evidence that he thought pleasure must be momentary, like the present moment. Thus, duration plays no role – neither as a criterion for pleasure nor in any argument about its temporal location.

For these reasons, I suggest translating *monochronos* as 'of a single time'. This respects the original semantic context without overstretching the metaphor and fits the Aristippan framework.[41] However, this is not a term Aristippus himself is likely to have used, as he showed no particular interest in time as such. More on this will follow. All pleasures, whether physical or intellectual, are of a single time – more precisely, being affected by pleasant things (*hēdupatheia*) is of a single time. This does not, by itself, indicate which time is meant. To clarify which time is meant, we must turn to the Aristippan context and consider the existence and essence of pleasure.[42]

Let us begin with the question: Are there past and future pleasures, or only present ones? Presentist views in modern metaphysics of time deny existence to past and future entities. Aristippus, by contrast, does not seem to deny that past and future pleasures exist. The passage suggests he takes their existence for granted, referring to them without qualification.[43] Nor does he reject the possibility of recalling past joys or anticipating future delights at present, implying personal persistence through time.

That past, present, and future pleasures are taken for granted in the testimony, needs qualification: pleasures are pleasures only insofar as the affection is present – that is, as there is current perception and ongoing smooth motion (DL II.85). Past pleasures were pleasures in a past present; future pleasures will

---

[41] I have corroborated with additional argument the criticism of the *LJS* rendering of '*monochronos*' as 'momentary' in Tsouna 1998, 15–7, and 2020, 383–4. Consider examples like *monoeidēs* (of a single kind; thus, uniform/simple), *monokerōs* (with a single horn), *monoklados* (single branch), *monomelēs* (consisting of a single limb), *monommatos* (one-eyed), *monostephanos* (having won a single contest), *monotonos* (of one tone in music), *monophthongos* (single vowel), *monochordos* (monochord).

[42] Tsouna 1998, 16, fn. 26, suggests the translation of *monochronos* as 'unitemporal and extended in the present', a rather long-winded phrase. In my view, neither present extension nor the uniqueness of the hedonic event is implied by the word *monochronos* itself.

[43] They are not being referred to in negative existential claims (as by modern presentists) but as parts of reality.

be so in a future present. Recollections and anticipations generate brand new pleasures in the present. To affirm the existence of all pleasures, we must expand the notion of the present beyond 'right now' to whatever time is co-present with a pleasant perception. We should understand that 'all pleasures are present' in this expanded sense.

Where does this leave *monochronos* and the time it refers to? Of which single time is the pleasant affective experience? The single time is not the present as a single, isolated part of time, beside the past and the future, but each particular present in which the affection was, is, or will be experienced – whether in the past, present, or future. Being *monochronos* is an essential feature of the pleasant experience that begins, occurs, and ends with the specific smooth motion that is caused in the subject by a present object. Each pleasant affection happens only once, when its relevant object is present – either perceived or represented in memory and anticipation. Since we always experience what we experience *now*, it follows that every pleasure is pleasure taken in a present object. We do not retrieve past pleasures as such, nor experience future ones in advance as they will occur; we have new pleasures in each present time in which the affection occurs.[44]

The uniqueness of pleasant affections can explain why there is no mention of memory or anticipation being pleasant *in the present*. The memory of past pleasures cannot reproduce those pleasures in the present because their unique kinetic nature cannot be replicated without the presence of the original pleasant object necessary for the same subjective affection. Past joys cannot be savoured now, as they are over and done with – unrepeatable perceptions tied to a particular moment. Pleasures experienced in the past present cannot be relived in their original form, since the object that caused the pleasure is no longer present, nor is the subject's being pleased, as a result, which depended on a specific, irreproducible motion. Yet, the cognitive capacity to recall pleasure remains intact, and it would be counterintuitive to deny that recollections can be presently pleasant. Thus, pleasure in memory must be understood not as a repetition of the past pleasure but as a new pleasure taken in the representation of the past event.[45]

---

[44] This is not the only way to understand recollection and anticipation of pleasure. For other models – for example, pleasant memory as retrieval of a past pleasant experience, potentially mixed with pains or pleasures from other sources, also based on character – think of Plato and Aristotle. See Warren 2014a, 129–74, on Platonic anticipatory and Aristotelian remembered pleasures and pains.

[45] That is how I take Diogenes Laertius' report (II.89): Aristippus' followers rejected pleasure from memory or anticipation, as the motion constitutive of pleasure ends with the event. The same applies to pain: Cyrenaics could mentally rehearse future evils without being affected as if the event were happening at present (Cic. *Tusc.* III.28–31; Graver 2002).

After introducing the nature of pleasure as *monochronos*, the source states that 'neither the memory of past enjoyments nor the hope for future ones were anything in relation to him' – not denying the possibility of presently pleasant recollections or anticipations, as explained above, but stressing that without (causing) present pleasure, they are nothing in relation to him. I take this to mean that they do not affect him (i.e., there is no present affection), rather than that they are of no concern or do not matter to him in any absolute sense: without pleasure, there is no good.[46]

Aristippus is then said to 'judge the good by the one and only criterion of what is present'. Given that this must be interpreted in a way consistent with the Aristippan tenet that pleasure alone is the good, the question arises whether 'the present' is to be understood within the sense that 'all pleasures – were – are – and will be – present' or in the narrow sense of now as *right now*. The sequence answers the question. The report shifts from memories and anticipations unaccompanied by pleasure at present, to past and future pleasures themselves, which are characterised as 'nothing in relation to him', too. In contrast to the expanded sense of the present of *monochronos*, the restricted scope of 'what is present' is evident from the reference to 'having enjoyed' and 'going to enjoy' – perfect and future tenses – implying that only pleasure felt now is 'something in relation to him' because it is affecting him.

The primacy ascribed to present pleasure is due to the fact that the present is the locus for all experience and affections. Past and future enjoyments are not devalued as irrelevant and unworthy of concern but are judged inferior in comparison to present hedonic affectivity.[47] As pleasures are the only good, and the present, narrowly construed, is the locus of experience, the good is one's present, particular pleasure – the one selected among current possibilities, whether pleasant or painful. Because the pleasant experience is the good one strives for, it is this particular present pleasure – not pleasure in general, nor past or future pleasures – that is Aristippus' primary concern.[48]

---

[46] The phrase *ouden estin pros tina* appears in various ancient Greek texts to indicate that something is not relevant to or does not concern someone – for example, Demosthenes, *Against Dionysodorus* 26.3; D.L. II.36 (Socrates on comic poets as not concerning us when they do not criticize a fault); D.L. VII.160 (Ariston of Chios stating that only the ethical field is *pros hēmas*); D.L. X.139 (Epicurus on death as nothing in relation to us, since what lacks perception is nothing in relation to us); *SVF* I.332 (Zeno on the things of this world); and Epict. *diss.* 1.29.25; 2.30.4; 3.16.16; 3.22.21; 4.5.33; 5.7.18; Epict. *Ench.* 1 (on what is not up to us as 'nothing in relation to us', such as the body, others' actions, or threats regarding things indifferent to us). When applied philosophically, the phrase depends on how the philosopher conceives 'what we are' and our corresponding function (*ergon*, see Epict. *diss.* 4.5.33).

[47] In the profligates' wording, 'nothing in relation to them' can indeed convey an absolute devaluation and disregard for the past and future.

[48] This need not make him a bundle of ever-changing desires, as O'Keefe 2002 portrays the Cyrenaics in explaining their focus on the present (i.e., because present desires change).

We need to examine whether the last part of A (2) confirms the reading so far. *To paron* (what is present) in A (2) refers to the affection of being pleased as the immediate sequence implies. Aristippus is not concerned with the metaphysics of time. 'Having had delight being not any longer' should rather be understood as saying it is *not any longer* a pleasant affect: it is not now a pleasure (though it was a pleasure previously). Because now is when we experience pleasures and pains, those that are currently occurring are to be distinguished among pleasures.

An explanation is added of why future pleasant experiences are considered nothing in relation to us: first, they are not yet pleasures at present, as per our reading; second, the future is *adēlon* (unclear). This can be understood both phenomenologically and epistemically. Phenomenologically, anticipated future experiences have not yet appeared and remain unrevealed, since the pleasant object is not present. Epistemically, the source suggests that anticipated affectivity lacks certainty. We cannot know what may intervene to prevent our expectations from being fulfilled – both whether the object will be there, and how it will affect us, if so. This is not a categorical statement, but depends on the circumstances. I do not doubt I'll enjoy ice cream tomorrow, since I fancy it – but some bad news I might hear could still affect its hedonic impact. In unstable situations, the ability to predict both the objects one will encounter and the affectivity they will elicit is compromised.[49] A (2) and B (3) will be compared in Section 2.2.3.

2.2.2 Aristippus' Paronism

Aristippus cannot be called a 'presentist' in the sense of modern temporal ontology. While he grants the present primacy as the locus of experience, he does not deny the existence of past or future pleasures and pains, whereas presentists claim that only present things exist. Matters become more intricate when we consider 'presentism' in contemporary ethical debates. The later Cyrenaics adopted a stance akin to time-relativity, in contrast to the Epicureans' time-neutrality. Revisiting Aristippus the Elder in light of these debates and portraying him as a precursor of the Cyrenaics may suggest a leaning toward time-relativity, but this does not withstand scrutiny in our

---

Instead, he could be someone who experiences life as a continuous flow of fulfillment, content with the currently pleasant objects that life presents him with – just as the anecdotes suggest. Since there is no evidence of 'present desires' in the sources but instead of 'present pleasures', I take the focus to be on fulfilling pleasure and not satisfying desire – similarly to Feldman's hedonism.

[49] See Section 3 for a discussion on how the agent delineates the present depending on varying inner and external contexts. The more unstable these contexts, the more one should narrow the focus to the present.

reading so far. The primacy of the present as the locus of experience is insufficient. More importantly, we lack textual evidence that Aristippus framed his leading question around whether the present adds value to pleasure or pain, all else being equal – the core issue in time-relativity versus time-neutrality, embedded in a maximizing framework. We show in Section 2.2.3 that maximization is not characteristic of the Aristippan model of well-being.

To paron in Athenaeus refers to (i) pleasant objects as efficient causes (e.g., Lais,[50] perfumes, fine clothes), and (ii) the resulting pleasant feeling, the *telos*, co-present with the objects. Both together constitute the complex content of *to paron* and aptly fit its grammar.[51] Though the referent of 'the present' (*to paron*) cannot be 'time' – for it would have to be *ho parōn chronos*, instead – the temporal sense is crucial since to be present to a person, something has to exist at the same time with the person. The relevance of the time aspect is further supported by the contrast of the present affections to past and future ones.

If those two referents – which support the narrow sense of the present – are taken as exhaustive, and although we do not take Athenaeus to be advocating exclusive care for the present, it might still appear that only the narrow present matters to Aristippus. But this is not the case. Aristippus also sees the co-presence of pleasurable object and feeling as 'material' for exercising mastery in the narrow present (iii). His aim is to train himself, in each moment, not to lose control or pursue pleasure's continuation (as Callicles does) or its maximization (like Protagoras' improved masses).[52] Mastery means a subtle combination of immersion and detachment. Xenophon, despite portraying Aristippus as indulgent (*Mem.* II.1.11), notes his idea of freedom as key to happiness.[53] Aristippus seeks a middle path – neither ruler nor slave – wandering as a stranger, a stance criticized by Xenophon.[54] Though the context is thoroughly political, this freedom also concerns pleasure: a balance between abstinence and excess, marked by lightness and detachment from the power and dominion of pleasure.[55]

---

[50] Lais of Corinth was a famous courtesan (*hetaira*) said to have been Aristippus' companion, to whom he refers in the anecdotes (see fn. 59).

[51] I mean that *to hēdu* or *to pathos tou hēdesthai/apolauein/tēs hēdonēs*, and *to paron* are grammatically fitting. When *telos* is addressed (e.g., D.L. II.66), being pleased should be taken as the end-result. As for the triad's third element, *to paron sōphronein* would fit grammatically, reflecting Aristippus' view of moderation as a kind of present gymnastics through pleasure.

[52] The assumption of the majority of interpretations that Aristippus was a maximizer is not grounded in textual evidence; see, for instance Annas 1993, 38, 447, Graver 2002, 162, O'Keefe 2002.

[53] Consider *hēper malista pros eudaimonian agei* (*Mem.* II.1.11-2), which Tsouna 2002 rightly interprets as evidence against Aristippus' anti-eudaemonism.

[54] See Urstad 2018 on a fine-grained analysis of the notion of freedom in Aristippus the Elder as reported in Xenophon's *Memorabilia*.

[55] This restraint, grounded in prudential reasoning, rejects the profligate's stance: though all pleasures are good, not all ways of enjoying them are. Some may cause harm in the present or

Maximus of Tyrus calls Aristippus moderate: to be precise, he says that Aristippus does not exercise less moderation (*sōphronein*) than Diogenes the Cynic, a paradoxical statement at first sight, given the gap between Aristippus' hedonism and Diogenes' asceticism:

> The famous Aristippus, who wore a purple robe and anointed himself with myrrh, exercised no less self-control than Diogenes; For if someone rendered the body capable (*dynamin sōmatos pareskeyasato*) of not being ruined by fire, they would, I believe, be confident enough to even throw themselves into Aetna. Similarly, the one who has prepared himself well with regard to pleasure (*pros ēdonēn pareskeyastai kalōs*) is not inflamed or burnt or melted away when one is in them [i.e., pleasures].[56]

As ever with analogies, it is crucial to identify the *tertium comparationis*. Maximus compares fire to pleasure, suggesting that just as we can train our bodies to endure fire – *per impossibile*, even Mount Etna's heat – we can likewise train ourselves to face pleasure without succumbing to its destructive effects. The analogy's point is not the impossibility of such training (the latter is presented to be possible), nor bodily focus in both cases (we train ourselves, not the body, in the latter), but the aim: exposure to the element without destruction. What does this mean for pleasure, if it is the only good? Think of debauchery causing future pain. Textual evidence confirms that Aristippus was not indifferent to future consequences.[57]

Aristippus immersed himself in pleasure with sober detachment, engaging without being overcome, possessing pleasures without being possessed.[58] His disciplined mastery enabled him to disengage at will, indicating a pursuit of control rather than mere maximization. Clement of Alexandria observes that Aristippus trained himself both through and within the experience of pleasure (*gymnazesthai di' autēs en autēi*), and characterizes his skill in navigating pleasure as a form of art (*technē*).[59] It is distinct from the technique Socrates imparts in *Protagoras* since aiming not at

---

future, while restraint builds lasting stability and capacity for pleasure, exercisable in any circumstance. One can be an optimizer, though not a maximizer.

[56] *SSR* IV A 58/ Mannebach 56: Maxim. Tyr. *Phil.* I.9.

[57] Xen. *Mem.* II.1.5 shows that Aristippus avoids adultery due to consequences; he prioritizes present pleasure but not at the cost of future harms – hardly a profligate indifferent to outcomes.

[58] On employing or having pleasure (and willingly ceasing pleasure) instead of being possessed by it, consider [Plut]. *Vit. Hom.* II.150 (*SSR* IV A 55/ Mannebach 30), D.L. II.69 (*SSR* IV A 87/ Mannebach 59); Athen. 544d, D.L. II.74–5 and Clem. Al. *Strom.* II.20.117–8 (all three in *SSR* IV A 96/ Mannebach 57D/ 57A/ 57B respectively), *Gnom. Vat.* 743, n. 493 (*SSR* IV A 97), Stob. *Ecl.* III.17,7 (*SSR* IV A 98/ Mannebach 55). His claim to 'possess Lais' is egotistic, though he had a long-term relationship with the famous hetaira and reportedly wrote two books about her.

[59] Clem. Al. *Strom.* II.20.117–8 (*SSR* IV A 96/ Mannebach 57B).

maximization but at establishing cheerfulness as a disposition in all contexts (see Section 2.2.3).[60]

Diogenes Laertius' doxography supports these points about *to paron*:

> He was capable of adapting himself to place, time, and person, and of fittingly playing the part under all circumstances; hence he was in greater favour with Dionysius than others, as he always made the best of everything that happened to him (*aei to prospeson eu diatithemenos*); for, he used to take pleasure in whatever was present, and did not go in for labouriously hunting down the enjoyment of things that weren't present (*apelaue men gar hēdonēs tōn parontōn, ouk ethēra de ponōi tēn apolausin tōn ou parontōn*). D.L. II.66.[61]

One who aims to live pleasantly with present enjoyable objects would undermine this goal by neglecting them for painful toil aimed at future gain. Such focus would forfeit immediate pleasures – and the chance to cultivate the right attitude through them for the sake of taking in pleasures in all contexts to the extent possible. This does not mean Aristippus always chose immediate pleasure: if a present pleasure risked serious future harm, he would forgo it and seek an alternative now.[62] His adaptability was key, including the ability to transform potentially painful experiences into pleasurable ones, to which we will return when analyzing the nature of pleasure and the cognitive element in Section 2.3.

We interpreted 'what is present' through Aristippus' preference for ordinary usage – eschewing philosophical refinements – in terms such as *telos* and *to paron*, the only appropriate methodology in his case. We concluded he values what is immediately accessible over what is absent. While we portrayed him as avoiding future calculations or maximizing pleasures due to lack of evidence – the usual form of prudentialism – we established a compatibility with concern for overall well-being: he cultivated a practiced balance of immersion in, and detachment from, present pleasure. We now turn to Aelian's report to explore possible motivations, as Plato did with hedonists in *Protagoras* and *Gorgias*.

---

[60] *SSR* IVA 98, Stob. *Ecl.* III.17,7 likens pleasure to a ship or horse – means we use to reach our goals, not something to avoid. If we press the analogy and pleasure as a means, Aristippus seems to have two goals; I argued for primary and secondary concerns to avoid this tension. The only goal is specific pleasure.

[61] The largest part of *SSR* IV A 51/ Mannebach 29 together with 54B. *Ta paronta* (plural of *to paron*) refers to present pleasurable things – not to pleasure as feeling, nor to abstract present time (for which the singular is used).

[62] Though some sort of quantitative reasoning may be at play here, it does not have to be shaped by a strictly speaking 'maximizing' agenda, for which see Section 2.2.3.

2.2.3 Aelian's Contribution

Aristippus' Present-Focused Therapeutic Policy

We have understood Aristippan *paronism* as a way of living that prioritizes present pleasures over past and future affective states, aiming at the person's relative good. Crucially, Aristippus distinguishes between what is at hand and what is unavailable, rather than between present, past, and future time.

The next step is to explore possible motivations behind his present-focused hedonism. As Athenaeus noted, some profligates emphasize the present while devaluing memory and future goals, pursuing immediate pleasures, a stance for which Philodemus, a later Epicurean, suggests one motive: a desire to escape the thought of inevitable death – an unphilosophical, anti-rational '*carpe diem*' that avoids pain and reflection alike.[63] We have already shown that Aristippus does not align with such uncritical and anti-rational hedonism and so his focus on the present must differ significantly in form and justification.

By analyzing Aelian's report – thus far set aside – we will develop what I call a 'therapeutic policy' as a charitable reconstruction of Aristippan motivation, before introducing three alternative motivations to explain a present focus, which, as far as the historical reconstruction is concerned, cannot withstand scrutiny.

Text B (1) presents Aristippus explicitly asserting – not merely implying – a particular stance toward past and future events. The passage does not advocate disregarding them altogether,[64] nor does it suggest we should avoid considering past affects or planning ahead to mitigate future pains where possible. Rather, Aristippus emphasizes avoiding unnecessary toil before or after events occur. This shifts the focus to painful past and future events, in contrast to Text A that centres on pleasant ones. Moreover, B (1) underscores the importance of *attitude*, unlike A. Aristippus does not deny the reality or badness of painful or potentially devastating events. Instead, he distinguishes between superior and inferior attitudes, recommending the former. He does so by using two cognate verbs derived from *kamnein* (to toil), each with a distinct prefix. First, one should not *epikamnein* (toil over) past painful events: a term appearing here for the first time in extant Greek, later attested in Cyril of Alexandria.[65] The other term, *prokamnein* (toil beforehand), is not unique to this passage. LSJ glosses it as 'to suffer at or after' and 'be distressed beforehand', but *kamnein* need not denote affective experience. In this context, it denotes cognitive toil or

---

[63] Phld. *De Elect.* XVII, and Indelli and Tsouna 1995 for commentary, 195–200.
[64] The normative aspect of his hedonism is clearly implied here – it's not just descriptive but prescriptive – even if the reports reviewed so far, which lack a theorist, do not state it explicitly. Tsouna 1995, however, initially denies any normative element in his thinking.
[65] Cyril. *in Jo. Ev.* I.297.11–2.

exertion. As Diogenes Laertius (II.66) notes, Aristippus would not strive through toil (*ponos*) for what is absent. This cognitive strain – whether directed backward or forward – may, however, cause affective strain and pain if it develops into rumination, anxiety, and depression.[66]

Will the recommended attitude affect the intrinsic value of past or potential future pains as they occurred or might occur? Will bad events become good if we refrain from ruminating on them? Absolutely not. Past pleasures *were* inherently good, and past pains *were* inherently bad, according to Aristippus. Nonetheless, the recommended attitude of 'not toiling' over past pains is advocated because it benefits the present and can enable a better shaping of future affectivity.

How is this possible? Excessive rumination on past events or overwhelming anxiety over future negative scenarios hinders one's capacity to assess and benefit from the present. Worse, individuals with tendencies of depression and/or anxiety who fixate on past sufferings and fret about gloomy future prospects often overlook the present positive elements and fail to invest in pleasurable experiences, their attention attracted by bleak aspects of the present reality. Psychological findings on depression and the affected individuals' negative cognitive schemas confirm that such individuals neglect the pleasant objects right before them and the goods they currently possess, missing the opportunity for potential relish in present pleasure, and instead grievously dwell on past failures (or what they took to be failures) and agonizingly fret about upcoming gloomy events.[67]

Aristippus, according to our reconstruction (see the third reference of 'what is present', Section 2.2.2), can identify a subtler failure, too: by missing current pleasant experiences, such individuals lose the chance to train themselves through these pleasures without becoming attached to the objects. Further consequences ensue: they do not merely anticipate negative outcomes but dwell on them now. Fixating on past failures, with fretting and rumination producing avoidable present pains, precluding available present pleasures by overlooking favourable aspects and projecting disaster, is a foolproof strategy

---

[66] Put differently: *ponos* (toil) may, but need not, be painful (*lypēros*). Lampe 2015, Tsouna 2020, and Warren 2014a translate correctly without reflecting on the affective and cognitive aspects involved.

[67] A self-schema is a complex set of beliefs and generalizations about the self – formed through past experience – lifelong, existential, and identity-shaping beliefs that pertain to specific domains (e.g., 'I am intelligent; 'I am socially awkward') that guide how new information about the self is processed. Due to active and deeply ingrained maladaptive beliefs like 'no one loves me', 'I am never successful at my work', 'being in a relationship always ends up giving me pain', coupled with biased attention and memory, the afflicted person will be attracted to past, present, and future pains rather than pleasures. On cognitive schemas, see Dozois and Beck 2008.

for lifelong frustration. Given all that, Aristippus' advice – though concerned with the present attitude toward past and future negative events – is clearly aimed at establishing overall well-being, not merely episodic, hedonic, fleeting moments.

Whereas Text A helped us define pleasure as essence and goal, B (1) recommends an attitude toward past and future pain, correcting the possible misleading impression from reading Text A in isolation that Aristippus offers no reflection on or concern for past and future affectivity; for to delineate the appropriate attitude is a serious concern.[68] Text B (2) provides a brief and enigmatic explanation for B (1): 'For (*gar*) such an attitude is a sign of cheerfulness and a proof of a gentle mind." What does it mean to say that avoiding dwelling on past pains or fretting about future ones is a sign of cheerfulness?[69] Had Aristippus aimed at the maximization of pleasure, what better moment than this to assert that acting as in B (1) would maximize overall pleasure? But he does not. Instead of making such a claim – or even speaking directly about pleasure as what one pursues through this strategy and exercise – the source explains the recommended attitude toward past and future pains with the aid of a disposition: it is a sign of cheerfulness. If the avoidance of fretting about past and future pains is recommended as a sign of cheerfulness without further qualifications, then the disposition of cheerfulness is recommended and praiseworthy as well.

A hedonist like Aristippus does not simply accept whatever pleasure comes his way from moment to moment on the grounds that all pleasure is good. He adopts a deliberate stance toward past and future and, in this respect, shows concern for them as well. Moreover, were he to embrace every pleasure indiscriminately, he would not elevate a disposition like cheerfulness as praiseworthy. Certainly, he aims at pleasures. While disinclined to formal distinctions, he appears to maintain two interrelated concerns, as introduced in Section 2.2.1. The first and primary concern is for pleasure as a present affection; the secondary concern is for cheerfulness as a cultivated disposition developed over time to enable the proper reception of pleasure in each moment. Cheerfulness and 'gentle spirit' manifest in not 'getting stuck' with past pains and future catastrophes independent of circumstances – step by step, day by day, by cultivating the right attitude toward past, present, and future pleasures and pains. To aim at pleasure in the present, with a view to the

---

[68] Unlike Lampe 2015, I do not detect an exercise already in Text A. It rather provides the basis for the therapeutic training recommended in Text B.

[69] *Deigma* (literally 'sample') and *apodeixis* stem from the verb *deiknysthai* (to show). The attitudes toward past and future pains serve as manifestations – as a sign and as evidence respectively – of a cheerful disposition and a gentle mind, not as mere appearances.

long-term establishment of enjoyment and contentment as a stable disposition, is an extraordinarily demanding ethical goal.[70]

If this reconstruction is correct, the character of Aristippan *paronism* emerges as pragmatic. More specifically, it is legitimate to call it 'therapeutic' – with due caution. Aristippus does not explicitly employ a medical analogy as later Hellenistic philosophers do. Yet in his pursuit of mastery over pleasure, he seeks to correct (potential) unhelpful tendencies and attitudes to different times, pains, and pleasures in order to establish present cheerfulness with the potential to permeate one's entire life: to be content and cheerful, as far as is possible, throughout life and in various contexts.

An additional passage in Aelian's same work (7.3) does support the therapeutic nature of his practical endeavor, though without providing any additional recommended strategies:

> Note that when some of Aristippus' companions lamented deeply (*odyromenōn barytata*), he addressed them with many other words as well, able to alleviate distress (*lypēs anastaltika*), and also said the following by way of preface: 'I have come to you not in order to grieve with you, but to stop you from grieving (*ouch hōs syllypoumenos, all' hina pausō hymās lypoumenous*).'[71]

Aristippus occasionally assumed the role of a therapist for others. This extract, together with Text B, which indicates that Aelian had access to more extensive sources than Atheneaus, place Aristippus in the tradition of *technē tēs alypias* (the art of alleviating distress),[72] suggesting his psychotherapeutic role was not a chance consequence of his significant focus on pleasures and, by extension, on pains. Although the word *technē* is absent, he is portrayed as skilled in the art of alleviating distress – a practical skill he shared with others who experienced severe distress. He engaged in dialogue with his distraught companions, speaking at length with the aim of relieving their suffering. There is nothing implicit or merely potential here, unlike in his talk about pleasures (in Eusebius). While doing so, he was notably able to detach himself from their distressing states – a

---

[70] This reconstruction of Aristippan thinking brings it surprisingly close to Epictetus' recommendation: 'Do not seek the occurrences to occur as you want but want the occurrences as they occur and your life will flow well' (*euroēseis*) (*Ench.* 8). I would understand the gentleness of spirit in B (2) as supported by the capacity to accept, transform, and, as far as possible, take pleasure in present circumstances, rather than being driven by an ever-changing bundle of desires for future fulfillment.

[71] *SSR* IV A 110.

[72] The tradition was initiated by the sophist Antiphon, who is reported to have been the first psychotherapist, practicing the art of alleviating distress (*technē tēs alypias*. DK 87 A 6) in the context of the medical analogy. On this, consider Furley 1992.

hallmark of a skilled therapist,[73] confident in his ability to alleviate their sadness, as the preface of his talk makes evident. The remainder of his address would likely have been invaluable.

Accordingly, we interpret these few lines as supporting a *therapeutic policy* that centres on the present without renouncing concern for overall well-being;[74] rather, it is precisely through this present-focused strategy that well-being is facilitated. Instead of 'going with the flow' with no compass beyond the immediate moment, we find a deliberate method, accompanied by specific recommended exercises.

By now, it is clear that Aristippus does not disregard past and future affectivity *tout court* but promotes a therapeutic policy that includes strategies for cultivating the right attitude toward them – such as not allowing past or future pains to overshadow present pleasures. Cicero's *Tusculan Disputations* III.13.28–9 presents another Cyrenaic method: premeditating future evils to reduce their impact.[75] Even if this belongs to the later Cyrenaic toolkit, as it is not attributed to Aristippus directly, it would be surprising – though not impossible – if his followers departed significantly from his practical recommendations. Be it as it may, though distinct, Cicero's and Aelian's techniques align, since Aristippus does not reject future consideration outright. Instead, he cultivates the right present attitude, including toward past and future, revealing his broader concern for shaping future present moments also through premeditation of future evils.

It is mutually enlightening to connect Aristippus' twofold concern to the discussion of 'the paradox of hedonism' in utilitarian hedonistic circles (by Mill and Sidgwick, for instance). Here is Mill's version:

> Those only are happy (I thought) (i) *who have their minds fixed on some object other than their own happiness*; on the happiness of others, on the improvement of mankind, even on some art or pursuit, followed not as a means, but as itself an ideal end. (ii) *Aiming thus at something else, they find happiness by the way. The enjoyments of life (such was now my theory) are sufficient to make it a pleasant thing, when they are taken en passant, without being made a principal object.* Once make them so, and they are immediately felt to be insufficient. They will not bear a scrutinizing examination. *Ask yourself whether you are happy, and you cease to be so.* The only chance is to treat, not happiness, but some end external to it, as the purpose of life. Let your self-consciousness, your scrutiny, your self-interrogation, exhaust themselves on that; and if otherwise fortunately circumstanced you will inhale

---

[73] His refusal to grieve with them does not imply a lack of empathy, especially given his aim to relieve their pain.

[74] Thanks to Nicholas Denyer for suggesting the term 'policy'.

[75] O'Reilly 2019 has persuasively argued in favour of the report's accuracy. See also Graver 2002.

happiness with the air you breathe, (iii) *without dwelling on it or thinking about it, without either forestalling it in imagination*, or *putting it to flight by fatal questioning.* (J. S. Mill (2018) *Autobiography*, ch.5, my italics and enumeration of points).[76]

Let us focus on the common distinction between primary and secondary concern in Aristippus' and Mill's hedonism, and discern the following points:

1. At first sight, the report has Aristippus disagreeing, recognizing specific pleasant experiences as the *telos*. The option is left open that *eudaimonia* is a second concern as argued in Section 2.2.1 and will be shown.
2. Mill concentrates on particular enjoyments, highlighting the disagreement between his view – that individual enjoyments should be taken *en passant* – and Aristippus' prioritization of present pleasant affectivity. However, Aristippus focuses not exclusively on specific objects and the emerging pleasures but on cultivating a long-term attitude toward pleasure. While prioritizing individual enjoyments, Aristippus' detached attitude prevents excessive focus on those pleasures, a stance Mill seems to echo in recommending a fleeting attitude toward these particular pleasures.
3. In the entire paragraph, and specifically in (iii), Mill discourages being excessively fixed on or obsessed with thinking and dwelling on what one gains in terms of individual pleasant experiences. That would be the best ticket for putting pleasure to flight and for the self-refutation of hedonism, a problem for which he offers a solution.

The therapeutic emphasis on the present aims to enhance overall well-being without invoking a *maximization model of well-being*, the latter of which is shaped by all following aspects: (1) The ultimate goal is the maximization of pleasures (and minimization of pains) in one's whole life, with the implication that (2) the maximizer welcomes (even) more pleasure. (3) The decision procedure is to calculate the hedonic consequences of one's actions and choose the one with the highest future score. (4) The maximizer always experiences the present as a means to the maximizing goal. (5) The key question about the present is what value it adds, if any, to goods (pleasures) and harms (pains), resulting in the theses of temporal neutrality versus relativity. Though Aristippus may seem a *prima facie* net-pleasure hedonist, who might agree with (1) but rejects (3) as self-defeating method, the attribution to him of *maximization* regarding any of the above aspects does not survive scrutiny: he neither compares pleasures nor aims at more, and he separates pleasure from *eudaimonia*, unlike Epicurus, remaining a Socratic in this respect. The greatest

---

[76] For another formulation of the paradox of hedonism, see Sidgwick 1907, 136, 403.

eudaimonia possible (Xen. *Mem*.II.1.11) equates to the greatest *euthymia* possible, as we will see, and the sufficient rather than the maximum is sought for.[77]

Turning to analogies in contemporary psychotherapy for the Aristippan policy, *Mindfulness for Life*, a course developed for all by the Oxford Mindfulness Centre and (interestingly) based on *Mindfulness-Based Cognitive Therapy for Depression* (Segal et al. 2013), exemplifies such a piecemeal approach. Practitioners become gradually accustomed to exercises that cultivate non-judgement, attentiveness, and presence in the current moment. Yet this focus on the present does not entail an abandonment of long-term aspirations: far from it. The expectation is no less than the gradual cultivation of a stable way of being – one that fosters overall well-being not through the calculation of hedons and dolors, but through the steady shaping of disposition.

To parallel the five points of the maximizing model, the euthymic model of well-being that underlies the Aristippan therapeutic policy (1) focuses on cultivating cheerfulness as an attitude; (2) it does not involve saying 'yes' to more pleasure; (3) instead of applying a life-wide art of hedonic measurement, each moment serves as training material for developing the right attitude and skill regarding pleasure; (4) the euthymist can experience the present without constant reference to an overall goal; (5) the key question is how to locate oneself – not goods and harms – in time by determining which present it is adaptive to attend to, given one's inner and external context, which is still to develop in Section 3. This model promotes specific attitudes toward past and future, not disregarding them, to support a content present disposition in each moment.[78]

We must now complete the analysis of Aelian's report. We have observed that Text B (1) refers to past and future events, not to past and future time in an abstract manner. B (3) clearly addresses temporality, with Aristippus recommending a focus on the present *day*, further narrowing it to the specific part of the day in which one thinks or acts. Understanding why Aristippus chose to specify a day or part of a day over other possible time periods is crucial.

Firstly, this choice suggests that the present is not merely a fleeting moment, but a duration of lived time, countering the notion of *monochronos* as describing

---

[77] On the contrary, Mill agrees with Bentham that the right action to perform is the one of the highest net utility, but rejects the how: instead of a hedonic calculus of felicity, he proposes rules of thumb and moral guidelines.

[78] Lampe 2015, 72, concludes that Aristippan presentism blends spiritual exercise with a prudential rule of thumb, but neither is doctrinally rigid. He argues that Aristippus sees no contradiction between this and his praise for education and virtue. While I think that the term 'spiritual' is misapplied – particularly the form of spirituality Hadot imposed and Lampe accepted – I agree that Aristippus' approach involves a kind of gymnastics focused on pleasure and the correct attitude toward it. I interpret Aristippus' paronism as a therapeutic policy, emphasizing a prudential concern for the entirety of life rather than merely a practical rule of thumb.

extremely short-lived or momentary pleasure. While a day is indeed a shorter unit of time than a life, a year, or a month, it is significantly longer than an instant. As a temporal unit of life, the day is marked by cyclical processes such as the periodicity of heartbeat, respiration, the sleep-wake cycle, and circadian hormone secretion (Fuchs 2018). These processes are completed within a day and repeat the next day, providing the day with a sense of completeness. A day has a concrete and objectively recognized beginning, middle, and end. Unlike the uncertain end of one's life, the end of the day is definitively located, irrespective of whether one survives the day or plans are completed or not. Aristippus advises taking life day by day, focusing on present concerns and troubles rather than worrying about past or future issues.

There is more to say about temporality in Text B (3). If the source refers to the present (time) as *to paron*, this would be the only extant report on Aristippus to do so. While we cannot rule out that possibility, the language and argument weigh against it. We take it to be more plausible that the nominalized adjective *to paron* denotes and collects all things that are now available. This reading avoids a shift from things that are past and future to abstract temporal periods – past, present, and future, and is reinforced by the verb *apollymi* in the argument that the past is not ours because it has perished: what is lost is not past time itself, but the pleasure once enjoyed. We should focus on the present because the past pleasures are gone, and the future remains uncertain. Another key detail supports this reading: the future is referred to as 'what is anticipated' (*to prosdokōmenon*). The implication is twofold: first, we anticipate not abstract time but desired events; second, the term implies a positive openness toward the future. Someone who has abandoned hope and focuses on the present out of despair would not use this neutral term. The Aristippan advice would be out of place in such context, since it cautions against tormenting oneself with anxious expectations. If all anticipations were grim, one might become consumed by worry to the point of no return – or worse, in a state of mental vulnerability or illness, choose death.

What does it then mean that one should focus on the daily cycle? The most plausible option is that Aristippus is a realist about how desired and anticipated events can develop or be thwarted due to numerous factors beyond our control. If this is the case, the motivation for focusing on the present cannot be to forget death and the fear of death by succumbing to present debauchery, nor to restrict oneself to the present as a result of pessimistically painting the future black or degrading one's capacity to calculate future pleasures and pains.[79] The

---

[79] I would agree with Warren 2014a, 195, that 'to take each day as it comes' is 'perhaps the best indication we have of time-relativity being embraced and promoted by a Cyrenaic' in Aelian – if there were evidence of Aristippus applying a hedonic calculus by comparing pleasures and pains based on their quantities. However, I find no trace of such a calculus, not even in a nascent form;

uncertainty of the future is part of the explanation for *paronism*, but it is neither the exclusive nor the predominant factor. Aristippus' *paronism* appears to be motivated primarily by his intention to focus on what he can control: not the future, but the cultivation of responsiveness to available pleasure and adaptability to present circumstances. This involves actively shaping experience, even transforming it from possibly painful to pleasant (see Section 2.3, and specifically 2.3.3, for the anecdotes).

Though temporality is addressed, the key Aristippan distinction is not between present, past, and future time, but between what is present to us and can be engaged with by us and what is not. By contrast, the attitude of the later Cyrenaics was shaped – perhaps predominantly – by their assessment that the future is uncertain.[80] In Aelian's report, however, the *decisive* point is that the present is ours, with all the implications we have indicated thus far, rather than that the future is uncertain. After all, future things are *anticipated* (*to prosdokōmenon*), in the sense of being expected, not despaired of. If despair were the attitude shaping and motivating Aristippus' *paronism*, another verb would have been used – such as in Epicurus, *Sent. Vat.* 17: *duselpistoumen*.

The thought in Text B (3) is evidently reminiscent of Stoicism, with two elements in particular evoking late Stoic tenets. First, only the present time is characterized as being *ours*.[81] Second and even more decisively – we are encouraged to shift our attention from longer to shorter spans of present time, especially by narrowing the present day down to the time in which we entertain a thought or perform an action. Although late Stoic exercises resemble Aristippan training in their focus on the present, the *retrenchable* present moment that the source clearly operates with goes beyond what Aristippus posited. Unlike the Stoics, Aristippus was not concerned with the physics or metaphysics of time, nor with their reflection in grammar.[82] There is no

---

on the contrary, there appears to be an aversion to this method. That said, Warren's interpretation remains unaffected for the Cyrenaics in general, apart from Aristippus.

[80] Rightly, Warren 2014a, 195.

[81] On the present time being ours, see Sen. *Brev. Vit.* and *Ep.* 1. Epictetus applied the distinction between what is ours and what is alien to his core distinction between what is up to us and what is not, though he does not refer to the present moment as within our power in the extant texts. Still, he calls the future indifferent and nothing to us (*Ench.* 32) and says we cannot decide for it (*aprohaireton, diss.* 4.10.8), hence it is neither good nor bad in itself. Marcus Aurelius does not describe the present time as ours. Though Epicurus calls the future neither fully ours nor fully not ours, to recommend a stance between confidence and despair (*Ep. Men.* 27), he does not make a point about the present, unlike Seneca or Aelian's report. For a sharp analysis and account of the differing views on the certainty of the future in Epicurus and the Cyrenaics, see Warren 2001 and 2014a.

[82] I considered the Stoic distinction between the present continuous and the present perfect as grounded in Stoic metaphysics of time and as underlying their understanding of (present) affections in Mouroutsou 2020.

indication that he conceived of the present as retrenchable or *plastic* – that is, as shaped by the subject's focal concerns – a Stoic concern that connects their physics of time to ethical practice.[83] His *paronism* and its therapeutic–policy character remain intact once we set aside these later accretions.

To immerse himself in present pleasure with control, Aristippus does not engage in any calculating business of comparing pleasures and pains among and with one another to increase the chances of greater future enjoyment. It is thus historically inaccurate to assume a hedonic calculus – or even its precursor – when there is no mention of hedonic quantities and comparisons.[84] What the sources do attest to is his unwillingness to risk missing what he has at hand, Aristippus gladly enjoys what is now available and the process of cultivating the right attitude and disposition toward pleasures. On the other hand, we have no textual evidence either that he hinted at the impossibility of comparison or commensurability between pleasures and pains. Nor would he call hedonic calculus a 'disease' in need of cure; Aristippus is not – and could not have been – an anti-utilitarian at heart, not even implicitly or naively.

He is clearly and decisively a non-maximizer. We detect in his untheorized hedonic *paronism* some hints of reasoning that could support an aversion to hedonic calculus – namely, his avoidance of present labour and toil (Xen. *Mem.* II.1.17ff.), which suggests a preference for a simpler approach to pleasure over complex calculation.[85] Rather than getting bogged down in comparing pleasures and pains, Aristippus capitalized on cultivating his attitude toward his being pleased now.[86] Although his being pleased now is both what he strives for and the criterion for goodness, it is the intricate blend of immersion and detachment that makes one's day; it seems to make Aristippus' day, for he believed that making the best of each present reality makes one's life happy too – or at least builds a path toward it. As argued in the previous

---

[83] See Mouroutsou 2020 on the plasticity of the present moment in his *Meditations* and the exercises of narrowing or expanding present time based on his state and moral progress. Consider Schofield's seminal 1988 article on the early Stoic theory of retrenchable present time. Lampe 2015, 64–73, rightly stresses the 'exercise' aspect in Aristippus' case but, following Hadot's fallible tendencies, blurs the boundaries by overlooking the crucial difference between Aristippus and the Stoics. See Mouroutsou 2024 for greater emphasis on divergences.

[84] Moreover, one should not assume maximization as the only theoretically available conception of rationality; if it is to be endorsed normatively, that requires argument – see Slote 1989 for an incisive critique. The way I reconstruct Aristippan *paronism* offers a non-maximizing example of prudential reasoning.

[85] Later Cyrenaics understand *eudaimonia* as nothing more than a sum of particular pleasures – they find it burdensome to attempt to achieve *eudaimonia* by eschewing present pleasures for the sake of future ones (D.L. II.90). (I read *eudaimonian poiountōn* rather than Dorandi's *mē poiounta* at the end of D.L. II.90; see Sedley 2017, 93).

[86] On Cyrenaic epistemology, see Tsouna 1998; for a succinct integration of Cyrenaic epistemology into their hedonism of particular pleasures as unrepeatable hedonic events, see Warren 2014b, 416–21.

section, he is no anti-eudaimonist. Certainly, he avoided venturing into calculating strategies and practiced his piecemeal approach.[87] Had he articulated an aversion to the hedonic calculation business successfully, he might have said (partly) what James Warren says when reflecting on the limits of prudential planning based on hedonic calculus:

> The calculation, for example, is itself likely to be of some hedonic cost in so far as it requires time and effort and, even if it is not itself a painful activity, precludes the performance of some other potentially more pleasant activity. Indeed, perhaps the procedure is sufficiently demanding that it will be better overall in hedonic terms sometimes not to engage in it and instead to make a choice based on much less accurate consideration.
>
> Warren 2014a, 116, n. 21.

Warren's words could be extended to support Aristippus' principal aversion: Aristippus shuns toil in general, under which the irksome business of hedonic calculus falls as a specific instance – though he would not engage in cost calculation in the quantitative manner suggested by the overall model in Warren's paragraph. Beyond this avoidance of toil, hedonic calculus is fundamentally incompatible with the therapeutic policy as we analyzed it – a pleasure-*technē not* aiming at *maximizing* pleasure, but at cultivating the contextualized right attitude to pleasure for the sake of pleasure in each and every present moment as far as possible. That he shows no interest in hedonic calculus provides an added reason for his lack of concern with the relevant debates – namely, that he expresses no explicit interest in supporting positions such as time-relativity (the primacy of the present over past and future when it comes to goods or harms) as opposed to time-neutrality (equal value of past, present, and future), unlike his followers. The emergence of that debate presupposes an articulated hedonic calculus, the dialectic between the Cyrenaics and Epicurus, and the question of the value of the present together with its maximizing framework.

We have interpreted Aristippus' claim that the future is 'unclear' as referring to future instances of the *pathos* of being pleased in Text A (2) and the fulfillment of anticipatory content in Text B (3), and analysed the phenomenological and epistemic aspects of unclarity in A (2), which B (3) notion of unclarity shares. The role of future uncertainty in Texts A and B may be construed differently in

---

[87] In *Mem.* II.1.11, Xenophon presents Aristippus as believing that his way of conceiving and exercising freedom leads most directly to *eudaimonia* (*malista pros eudaimonian agei*). Cicero (*Tusc.* III.28–31) reports that the Cyrenaics – though not explicitly Aristippus the Elder – practised pre-rehearsal of future evils, imagining misfortunes as real possibilities to lessen the shock and thus the pain if they occur. See Graver 2002 on this and Sedley's insightful reading of the strategy as lowering hedonic expectations to disarm the impact of severe future pain (2017, 99).

various presentisms. The Cyrenaics considered hedonistic calculations for prudential planning regarding the future; the most prominent – or notorious – representative of a pessimistic, if not depressive, outlook was Hegesias. However, we find no evidence of either hedonistic calculations or a pessimistic orientation in Aristippus himself, the founder. Accordingly, we do not attribute his aversion to comparing and calculating future pleasures to a pessimism rooted in failed hedonistic strategies aimed at securing overall happiness – alas, the future is unclear. Rather, we understand it as arising from his commitment to a therapeutic policy that – as reconstructed – is incompatible with a hedonic calculus and the maximizing framework to which it belongs.

According to the anecdotal material, Aristippus' attitude toward future pleasures resembles that of an optimistically inclined realist. He acknowledges the possibility of abundant future goods and pleasures that may indeed await us. We not only anticipate them with hope but also cultivate an attitude that prepares us well to receive them when they occur. At the same time, he recognizes that many factors beyond our control may intervene. Instead of squandering the present moment and its potential for precious training on speculative anxieties, Aristippus advocates focusing on the pleasure at hand, mastering it, and finding fulfillment in it. His lack of concern over whether specific future events will unfold as hoped does not reflect indifference to the future; rather, it signals a divergence from the hedonic calculus as the appropriate means to that end.

Further Motivations for *Paronism*

We have analyzed Aelian's report and made a case for an Aristippan *paronism* as a 'therapeutic policy': aligned with prudential concern for overall well-being, though not involving a hedonic calculus aimed at maximizing overall pleasure and minimizing overall pain. Let us now consider three additional motivations for the Aristippan *paronism* as a way of life: two categories of excruciating states: (i) suffering from distressing mental states such as depression and anxiety, (ii) suffering from devastating external circumstances and (iii) abandoning a 'narrative conception of the self' as extended through time. None of these were adopted by Aristippus himself. For (i) and (ii), Aristippus did not suffer from such misfortune and addressed his advice to all people, and not only those suffering from such misfortune. Nonetheless, a focus on what is present – particularly present pleasures – can be, and indeed is, integral to therapeutic strategies and developing coping mechanisms for people who suffer from such misfortune.

(i) Mental Struggles

Clinical literature and practice highlights that grounding patients in the present moment and shifting their attention from thinking about their entire life to being engaged with a current activity is an effective therapeutic strategy for a variety of ailments. This approach, employed in various therapies, including meditation-based cognitive therapies and cognitive behavioral therapy for depression,[88] focuses on the immediate moment – whether it is the immediate problem or emotion the therapist and the patient focus on, or the therapist–patient relationship as it develops currently.[89] For those suffering from depression, particular attention in various interventions is given to pleasurable moments, either past or present, due to their struggle with anhedonia.

We do not have evidence of Aristippus struggling with depression or anxiety, conditions where one uncritically fixates on the past or quickly anticipates a bleak future. These mental states can drive one who aims at improvement to focus on the present moment and current activities, offering a reality check about things that are available instead of fleeing into the black spirals of negative ruminations about things that are absent in a period in which someone is susceptible to erroneous thinking processing. The reports portray Aristippus as consistently cheerful, suggesting that curing emotional distress was not his motivation for focusing on the present. His goal was to cultivate cheerfulness as an attitude and disposition, not merely as a transient mood in each fleeting moment without the need for therapeutic intervention. Moreover, in Text B (1), Aristippus recommends that all people avoid toiling over past or future pains, rather than addressing a mentally burdened population.

(ii) External Crises

A further possible motivation for making present pleasure the focal concern may arise when one is undergoing a period of external crisis. In such circumstances, the emphasis on the pleasure of the day – if indeed any pleasure is to be found – becomes intelligible as not merely a preference but as the only reasonable and pragmatic strategy for survival. Consider, in this light, the counsel offered by the ghost of Darius to the Elders' chorus in Aeschylus' *Persians*, after he has laid bare the catastrophic misfortunes suffered by the Persian forces – the utter ruin of their troops at the hands of the Greeks, the crop of calamities and harvest of tears. In the face of such overwhelming ruin, when evils lie both behind and ahead – past evils

---

[88] In *Mem.* II.1.11, Xenophon presents Aristippus as believing that his way of conceiving and exercising freedom leads most directly to *eudaimonia* (*malista pros eudaimonian agei*). Cicero (*Tusc.* III.

[89] 28–31) reports that the Cyrenaics – though not explicitly Aristippus.

now endured and future evils looming though still unspoken – the only sensible course of action, he advises, is to turn attention to the pleasures of the day, making use of their existing wealth to find whatever solace may be now possible amidst the wreckage.[90]

Thus, the Aristippan motto 'now is the end' is not entirely foreign to ancient Greek intellectual thought; it surfaces in Attic tragedy, though typically in contexts of acute suffering that prompt a turn toward present pleasures. While the traditional maxim 'call no man happy until he is dead' – which demands the evaluation of an entire life to determine *eudaimonia* – dominates classical reflections on happiness, it was not the only view circulating within the cultural milieu. For instance, beyond the wartime setting of *Persians*, *Bacchae* 902–11 offers a series of illustrations of happiness: finding safety after a sea storm, prevailing in toil, and enjoying the pleasure of hopes, whether fulfilled or not. The chorus concludes by calling truly happy (as culmination; see Dodds 1960 *ad loc.*) those who find happiness from day to day (*kat' hēmar*).[91] From this parallel I draw two conclusions: first, Aristippus' *paronism*, especially his emphasis on the pleasure of the day, was not a novel idea but rather an accentuated aspect within the cultural environment of Athens; second, *paronism* and *carpe diem* alike should not be reduced to impulsive indulgence in food, drink, or sex.[92]

The two assumptions I have explored to explain an Aristippan hedonic paronism involve disruptions to life's continuity: either within the inner mental sphere – such as debilitating moods or affective disorders like depression or anxiety – or in the external world, through extreme calamities like

---

[90] the Elder – practised pre-rehearsal of future evils, imagining misfortunes as real possibilities to lessen the shock and thus the pain if they occur. See Graver 2001 on this and Sedley's insightful reading of the strategy as lowering hedonic expectations to disarm the impact of severe future pain (2017, 99).

scapes calamity: see the chorus in Eur. *Ba.* 910–1 and Hecuba in Eur. *Hec.* 627–8, *kat' hēmar bios eudaimōn / kat' hēmar mēden kakon*. I am not concerned with all hedonistically inclined tragic passages, nor with every instance of *carpe diem* (Dodds 1960, ad Eur. *Ba.* 424–6; Rohland 2023, 24, n. 98), but with those that explicitly invoke the unit of present time – specifically the day – in relation to pleasure. The *Persians* lines are exemplary in this regard, whether or not we see them as reflecting the hedonistic Sardanapallus epitaph or a more widespread Greek conception of the so-called 'Eastern' hedonism (Rohland 2023, 47, n. 28).

[91] Consider *Matthew* 6.34, where – after urging the pursuit of the heavenly kingdom over earthly concerns – he advises: 'Do not worry about tomorrow, for tomorrow will worry about itself. Each day has enough trouble of its own." This too confines attention to the present day. Rather than dismissing *paronism* as mere common sense lacking a grounded ontology of time – because it appears in religious, literary, and wisdom texts – we argue for its genuine philosophical significance in shaping answers to how one should live and relate to their past, present, and future.

[92] 'Wait until the end' was the dominant motto, especially in Solon's dialogue with Croesus (Hdt. I.30–3), where he urges focusing on the end of things, not the present goods (I.33, 4–5), with Aristotle (*EN* I.10) sharing this view.

war, or simultaneously in both domains. While such disruptions are not explicitly mentioned as actually motivating Aristippus, they could – at least temporarily – justify an Aristippan-like present-focused stance that – now is the end and the only concern'. Crucially, the Aristippan therapeutic policy as we presented it is not merely a remedy for severe afflictions or a strategy to preserve sanity in crisis; it is a policy for life, not a response to a mental struggle or devastation alone.

(iii) Non-narrative Types

Last but not least, there is a further possibility worth considering as a candidate for an Aristippan *paronism* – one that extends beyond extreme cases of disruption and is admittedly at odds with the concept and experience of a continuous life familiar to most of us. Though not proposed as an explanation of the historical Aristippus' focus on the present, Galen Strawson has articulated a form of time- and self-experience he calls 'episodic'. In his 2004 work, he challenges the widely held view – both descriptively and normatively – that human lives are, or ought to be, lived as continuous narratives. Two assumptions typically go unquestioned in everyday discourse and in much of philosophical thought: that we live our lives by constructing a continuous personal narrative (the descriptive hypothesis), and that we ought to live in accordance with such a narrative (the normative hypothesis). Against this, Strawson argues for the reality and legitimacy of an episodic type of experience of time and selfhood, which he distinguishes from the diachronic or narrative types. In diachronic self-experience, 'one naturally figures oneself, considered as a self, as something that was there in the (further) past and will be there in the (further) future'; by contrast, in episodic self-experience, 'one does not figure himself, considered as a self, as something that was there in the (further) past and will be there in the (further) future'.[93]

Strawson articulates the stakes as follows:

> It's just not true that there is only one good way for human beings to experience their being in time. There are deeply non-Narrative people and there are good ways to live that are deeply non-Narrative. I think the second and third views [the second view is the falsehood of the descriptive and the truth of the normative thesis, and the third option has both descriptive and

---

[93] Strawson 2004, 430. Though both types may be present in the moment, they are so differently: episodics inhabit the present in terms of self-experience. Strawson 2004, 431f., eloquently narrates misunderstandings between episodic and diachronic types. Compare Strawson 2004, 433, with Aristippus' qualified attention to past and future. Yet Strawson, due to a metaphysical stance Aristippus does not share, goes further: 'I do not have any great or special interest in my past. Nor do I have a great deal of concern for my future." According to my reconstruction of Aristippan therapeutic policy, there is serious concern, though secondary, for overall well-being.

normative theses true] hinder human self-understanding, close down important avenues of thought, impoverish our grasp of ethical possibilities, needlessly and wrongly distress those who do not fit their model [...].[94]

Though our Aristippus appears to be not much interested in fine philosophical explanations and self-reflection, unlike Galen Strawson who makes a case for his own typology, he does seem to presuppose the persistence of personal identity through a life (very clearly in Text A (2)), though one could not guess how he would react if he were pressed on the point.

Could his stance plausibly lie somewhere along the spectrum between episodic personality and continuous life-experience – especially given that a spectrum theory of personality traits does not rely on a pure-cases model, and the episodic typology is neither absolute nor exceptionless? Although difficult to determine, Aristippus does seem to presuppose the persistence of personal identity through a life, most clearly in Text A (2). Moreover, we have articulated a space for prudential reasoning about overall well-being in his case, albeit not grounded in a maximizing model of well-being.

In Section 2.4, we will consider an episodic, unphilosophical type as depicted in the *Philebus*, to contrast this figure with the Aristippus whose views we will by then have reconstructed. For now, I hope to have shown that Aristippan *paronism* is not reducible to profligacy, and that the therapeutic orientation provides a compelling and robust motivation for it – one that withstands scrutiny more successfully than alternative perspectives.

Conclusion

I have attributed a pragmatic – and specifically therapeutic – character to Aristippan hedonic *paronism*. Aristippus does not engage in the kind of temporal ontology modern and contemporary philosophers articulate. Rather than advancing a subtle philosophical theory, he operates with everyday reasoning: present things are available and within reach, in contrast to the absent pleasant and painful objects. That something is available – secondarily, due to temporal proximity – wins out, while absence – secondarily, due to temporal distance – is what disqualifies.

This distinction between what is at hand and what is not underlies Aristippus' implicit aversion to a systematic hedonic calculus. On my reconstruction, he avoids missing the chance to benefit from what is now available by turning his

---

[94] Strawson 2004, 429. He later critiques narrative types' tendency to generalize their experience 'with that special, fabulously misplaced confidence that people feel when, considering elements of their own experience that are existentially fundamental for them, they take it that they must also be fundamental for everyone else." (439). In an era marked by increased acceptance of otherness – or subtler political correctness – we aim to be more reflective and accommodating.

attention to what is absent. A practical sense of reality keeps him grounded; concerns about temporal ontology do not occupy him. His way of pursuing *eudaimonia* involves continuity, built moment by moment. He is neither heedlessly unreflective nor irrational – he does not aim to forget tomorrow by gratifying every impulse. What matters for him is the 'bird in the hand': the currently available pleasant object and the pleasure arising from it. This is the material for his virtue of mastery – a subtle combination of immersion and detachment.

I have now addressed Mann's challenge by offering a plausible justification of the Aristippan way of life, without recasting Aristippus as a theorist.[95] The therapeutic and piecemeal character of his strategy deserves emphasis, especially in contexts of crisis and disruption of life's continuity, and for individuals who face, either episodically or persistently, the challenge of emotional distress. Yet Aristippus' contribution does not end there. I have read him as offering an effective critique of the limitations of prudential reasoning that relies on hedonic calculation.[96] That said, his 'therapeutic policy' does not reject prudential reasoning, but reframes it within a new model: the euthymic model.

2.3 Cognitive Elements in the Experience and Concept of Pleasure

This section adds a fourth point about the nature of pleasure to the three discussed in Section 2.2.1 – namely, its cognitive character. It seeks to draw some further conclusions about what it means to take pleasure according to Aristippus and show that 'pleasure is a perceived smooth motion' does not exhaust his account of its nature. It will rectify a widely accepted assumption about Aristippus, often taken for granted without critical examination, that he thinks of pleasure merely as a sensory experience: a simple feeling or sensation. I will challenge this assumption by decoding the meaning of taking in present pleasure as it falls upon one (D.L. II.91) and emphasizing the cognitive functions integral to the experience of pleasure. Moreover, I will demonstrate that, for Aristippus, as for the later Cyrenaics, pleasure is not merely sensory but fundamentally attitudinal and involves a significant cognitive element. Having carefully distinguished Aristippus from the later Cyrenaics in Section 2.2 to avoid attributing to him a hedonic calculation as a subsequent development in the dialectic between Epicurus and the Cyrenaics, this section will explore a

---

[95] 'There is nothing to Aristippus' philosophy, besides the way he lives his life. That life is not to be explained, but shown. That life is not to be given a positive justification.' Mann 1996, 119.

[96] See Warren 2014a, 186–96. He carefully appreciates both Cyrenaic and Epicurean schools, noting they are not diametrically opposed but shaped by key decisions: the Cyrenaics accept all pleasures – leading to lost confidence in sustained happiness – whereas Epicurus limits desires to natural and necessary ones, allowing moderate future confidence.

topic that reveals a continuity between the founder and his followers. This continuity stems from discussions about pleasure found in Plato's *Philebus*; Aristippus functions as the connecting bond that mediates those to his followers.[97]

In Plato's *Philebus* 20–2, Protarchus and Socrates examine three human lives: the life of pure pleasure, that is, pleasure unmixed with any cognitive element, then, the life of pure intelligence, that is the life that is uncontaminated by the slightest portion of pleasure (or pain), and finally, the life in which pleasure and intelligence are mixed. Our task in this section is to show that the Aristippan life is not a life of pure pleasure as defined in the above *Philebus* context, that is, as excluding cognitive functions and elements.[98]

2.3.1 Taking in Pleasure 'As it Falls Upon One'

The Cyrenaic notion of taking pleasure as it falls upon one, often cited from Diogenes Laertius, remains understudied: 'It suffices even if one pleasantly recovers for the duration of the one pleasure that falls upon one (*prospiptousan*).'[99] This statement follows the claim that the Cyrenaics assign a pleasant life to all wise individuals and a painful life to fools – though only for the most part. It suggests that, regardless of broader claims about a pleasant life as a whole, it is enough to take in the specific pleasure at hand.

One might be tempted to interpret this as a passive acceptance of pleasure, as if it simply falls into one's lap, requiring no effort. However, such a reading oversimplifies the process. Like all hedonists and non-hedonists alike, Aristippus must actively choose among present experiences, discerning which are worthy of attention. At any given moment, multiple stimuli compete for our awareness, each capable of eliciting pleasure or pain – or both, in different respects. The act of recognizing and attending to pleasure, therefore, is far from passive; it requires cognitive engagement, including attention, discernment, and judgment.

---

[97] By addressing and correcting the philosophical misunderstanding, we also acknowledge that suchlike misrepresentations have permeated various strands of the tradition and have influenced interpretations even within modern ancient – and modern – philosophy quarters. Consider Feldman 2004, 31.

[98] For our purposes, the precise details of Plato's argument are irrelevant (see Mouroutsou 2021). We focus on a life of pure pleasure, not whether Aristippus would be refuted by Plato's argument, but whether he genuinely represents such a life as Plato considers.

[99] *Arkei de kan kata mian tis prospiptousan hēdeōs epanagēi* (D.L. II.91). The intransitive *epanagein* is particularly intriguing in this context. According to *LSJ*, its meaning varies depending on usage, encompassing 'withdraw', 'return', 'turn back', or 'restore one's health'. I have rendered it as 'recover', which supports an interpretation of pleasure as the restoration of our natural state.

To recognize something as pleasant and let the pleasure it causes fall upon oneself involves a complex cognitive process. Given differences in temperament and mental states, the same experience may be pleasurable to some and distressing to others. A person inclined toward pessimism or struggling with depression may find it difficult – or even impossible – to focus on something pleasant, instead dwelling on an unpleasant aspect of their circumstances. That summer and holidays are approaching may bring joy to some, while for others, it may evoke distressing associations. In this regard, Aristippus appears to navigate pleasures with deliberation, remaining alert and attuned to what genuinely provides enjoyment. As he managed well whatever befell him in D. L. II.66, he seems to have managed well the pleasures that occurred by being alert and attending to and recognizing the present object that caused the respective pleasure.[100] His approach is not that of a profligate surrendering to whatever bodily sensation arises before moving on to the next.

Aristippus seems to advocate cultivating a mindset where one's attitude toward pleasure matters more than its specific content in two ways: (i) Taking pleasure in potentially pleasant things depends on one's trained, deliberate attitude – both in choosing what to attend to and in resisting distractions from painful objects, whether present, past, or future. For example, approaching a holiday rightly makes it a pleasure, a smooth motion. (ii) Although all pleasures are good, the attitude one holds while experiencing or thinking about them can be better or worse: being ruled by present pleasures or being overly focused on past or future pains as overshadowing present pleasures is misguided. Though we distinguish attitude and content for the sake of the exposition, attitude is not merely an add-on, but both governs and constitutes the content and experience of pleasure.

This emphasis on attitude, however, does not mean that Aristippus endorses a fully-fledged attitudinal hedonism, in which pleasure is determined by a propositional attitude, as defended by Feldman 2004. Rather, his approach underscores the cognitive effort required to experiencing (past, present, and future) pleasure at present. Given the subtlety and complexity involved in attaining such pleasures, we have strong grounds to reject a simplistic sensual hedonism for Aristippus. Contrary to accounts that emphasize his pursuit of bodily pleasures, it is plausible that the later Cyrenaics, in their debates with the

---

[100] Diogenes Laertius uses the same word (*prospiptein*) for all things that befell Aristippus that he managed well. The subject of *prospiptein* in the later passage is each single pleasure (II.66: *to prospeson/ prospiptousan*, II. 91). Lucian (*Vit. auct.* 12, *SSR* IV A 59), though caricaturing Aristippus as inebriated and unable to participate in the dialogue, supports the idea that Aristippus collects pleasure *from everything* (*pantachothen eranizesthai tēn hēdonēn*), which can only result from a prolonged education and cognitive exercise.

Epicureans, reinforced this emphasis on bodily affectivity over intellectual pleasures.[101]

2.3.2 Cognitive Elements in the Cyrenaic Notion of Pleasure

Pleasure has a twofold meaning in both English and Greek (*hēdonē*): it can refer either to the subjective feeling of pleasure or to the pleasant thing or activity that causes it. In English, compare 'the pleasure is all mine' with 'cycling and swimming are my pleasures'. Plato and Aristotle similarly distinguish between pleasure as being pleased and the pleasant thing that causes it, reflected in *hēdesthai* (verb) and *to hēdu* (noun).

From pleasure as a smooth perceived motion – the subjective experience – we now turn to the pleasant thing that causes it. This recalls the twofold meaning of *telos*: as the end of an efficient causal chain (sense one),[102] and as the goal we pursue (sense two). Within the current causal framework, the pleasant thing functions as the efficient cause of the subjective pleasure, the latter of which is a *telos* in sense one.

With this in place, I will continue to challenge the oversimplified view of Aristippus as a profligate sensualist by first examining Cyrenaic doctrine before turning to him specifically. The key sources are Diogenes Laertius and Plutarch's *Table Talk* V.

The Doxographical Report

In his doxographical summary of Cyrenaic views, Diogenes Laertius includes the following report: 'They say that pleasures do not arise from mere sight or hearing alone (*kata psilēn tēn horasin ē tēn akoēn*); to illustrate, we enjoy listening to those imitating laments, but not pleasantly to those truly lamenting.' (D.L. II.90)

Diogenes discusses the emergence (*genesis*) of pleasures, using *kata* to indicate efficient causality. However, he does not present a general theory of pleasure's origin, as not all pleasures arise from sense perception. For instance, seeing a person one is infatuated with or hearing the clinking of beer glasses can evoke pleasure, just as an aesthetic experience can. His report thus concerns the occurrence of pleasures stemming from perception, whether they could be registered as bodily or intellectual.

---

[101] Remember the intellectual infatuation with Socrates as an intellectual pleasure among the frequent bodily pleasures reported. Consider D.L. II.87, Cicero, *Luc.* 139, Lactant. *Div. inst.* 28.3, 34–7.

[102] Present pleasures and pains can themselves have effects, and Aristippus considers future consequences. That said, his motto remains 'now is the end' and he thus focuses on the present pleasure as the end, though not necessarily the ultimate end.

However, mere sight and hearing alone do not fully explain pleasure's genesis. While they play a causal role, Diogenes' example highlights how identical perceptions (lamenting, for instance) can cause opposite affective effects – pleasure or pain – on different occasions.[103] This suggests an additional factor at play: we can perceive a sensible object, such as sight or sound, though not pleasant or painful in itself, as pleasant or painful – 'we enjoy listening', as the source says – when a cognitive element is added to perception. This cognitive element might be a thought independent of perception or a cognitive aspect integral to it. This source pleads for the latter, distinguishing between listening pleasantly and not pleasantly. Two kinds of perception, not independent thoughts, are highlighted: we listen to something *as* a pleasant imitated lament or *as* a painful genuine lament. The affective perceptual experience is intrinsically shaped by cognition, forming one unified affection.

If this is the case, the determining factor is how we interpret the same sight and sound of someone weeping – whether we perceive it *as* a staged performance or *as* genuine distress. The crucial thoughts concern our understanding of what we perceive. In the former case, pleasure arises from the awareness that the experience is theatrical. Compare how Aristotle's *Poetics* explains aesthetic pleasure through learning from representations in tragedy, since learning is inherently pleasant. (I do not claim that the Cyrenaics were influenced by Aristotle, nor summarize his theory here.) In contrast, if we believe the suffering is real, we experience pain. Again, this understanding carries cognitive content: we sympathize with human suffering.

Thus, what generates pleasure or displeasure is not the event's objective nature but how we perceive it – even if that perception is mistaken. For instance, if we wrongly take staged tears to be real sorrow, we may feel distress, which, per the Cyrenaics, will fade once we realize the truth. Conversely, if we mistakenly enjoy something as a spontaneous performance, discovering the person's real suffering will shatter our pleasure.

From Diogenes Laertius to Plutarch

(i) Preliminary Remarks and the Problem in Quaes. Conv. *V.1*

The introduction at Plutarch *Quaes. Conv.* 672D–673B establishes the thematic framework for all subsequent inquiries in Book V: the distinction between bodily pleasures and pleasures of the soul, the latter involving minimal or no bodily engagement. It also identifies the opponents: the Epicureans, portrayed

---

[103] *Ahēdōs* means 'not pleasantly', including neutrality and pain, in accordance with the Cyrenaics' three states: pleasure, pain, and neutrality.

as those who reduce the soul to a passive mirror of the body which merely reflects bodily sensations and adds pleasure or pain to accompany them. Allegedly, they fail to account for the soul's distinct and independent delight. Plutarch insists that the pleasures of the soul arise when symposiasts, having satisfied bodily needs, pursue intellectual pleasures that lift their thought (*dianoia*, 673A12).[104] These are furthest from bodily pleasures and satisfy a love for spectacle and wisdom without causing 'smooth motion in the flesh' or 'removing bodily pain', both allusions to the Epicurean view in *Kyria Doxa* 3.

The first problem for this framework (V.1.673 C–674 C) is to explain why we enjoy listening to imitations of anger, pain, or fear rather than becoming distressed, yet find it unpleasant when people manifest those genuine emotions. The question parallels the phenomenon in Diogenes' report but serves a different purpose: Plutarch does not analyze the generation of pleasure in Epicurean and Cyrenaic theories but rather classifies aesthetic pleasures as distinct pleasures of the soul, which he claims Epicurean theory cannot accommodate. Worse for the Epicureans, the rival hedonists they repudiate – the Cyrenaics – have understood these pleasures precisely. Plutarch, known for using the Cyrenaics to sharpen his polemics against the Epicureans, employs this tactic extensively in *Adversum Colotem*. Given both the playful nature of *Table Talk* and his broader philosophical agenda,[105] we must approach his account with caution – he is not committed to quoting philosophers with accuracy.

Plutarch focuses on artistic representation: seen sights and heard sounds (*theamata* and *akousmata*), just as in Diogenes' examples. He immediately reveals his explanation for the pleasure we take in artistic imitation (673D–E): we naturally love reasoning and art and therefore admire all successful products of reasoning and art more than natural products. What is naturally akin to us attracts us effortlessly (673F4–5) and, by implication, pleases us. Admiration is another source of pleasure, a theme sustained throughout the discussion.[106]

He examines theatre and plastic arts: theatre involves both sights and sounds, while the latter focuses on visual representation.[107] When we perceive a genuinely angry or sad person, believing them to be so, we are distressed. Plutarch does not explain this reaction explicitly but likely assumes that shared human

---

[104] As a Platonist, Plutarch knows the metaphysical and epistemological implications of *dianoia* but also uses it informally for 'thought', mind, or even interchangeably with the soul.
[105] Consider Kechagia 2011 on the combination of play and earnest in this work.
[106] See 673D11–2 which couples having affinity – not pleasure – while admiring, though what is akin is pleasant in itself (consider Arist. *Rh.* I.11 and compare *Quaes. Conv.* 674a9–10); Also, Parmeno's pig is admired (674B10).
[107] The Greek is slightly confusing. Though it seems to separate heard sounds from seen sights, both are integral to theatre. We hear actors' voices and see their expressions, gestures, and entire behavior on stage (*kai tas diatheseis*, 673D3). Angry and sad people, acting or not, are visually perceived in theatre and life (*horatai*, 673F7).

affections and movements cause us to respond sympathetically. Seeing someone dying or sick saddens us, whether due to awareness of human mortality, concern for the individual, or other reasons. In contrast, artistic representations of these affections – whether staged performances or painted and sculpted figures – please us. Our affinity for creations shaped by reason and art means that the more subtle, persuasive, and skillful the imitation, the more gladly we admire what we see and hear.

(ii) Plutarch's Report on the Cyrenaics

Plutarch introduces the Epicureans' rivals and attributes a general statement to them. My translation includes interpretative remarks in square brackets with two alternative readings (A) and (B) which I will consider below:

> This [that we take pleasure in artistic representations, though we would be distressed at the sight or the sound of a sad, angry, or withering person], I said, is a really strong proof according to the Cyrenaics against you Epicureans, that
>
> (A) [the subjective feeling of] pleasure (*to hēdomenon*) in the sounds and sights is not about the perception of sight nor about the perception of hearing but about our mind;
>   [or]
> (B) what takes pleasure (*to hēdomenon*) in the sounds and sights is neither in (the field of) the perception of sight nor in (the field of) the perception of hearing but in our mind;
>
> for a ceaselessly cackling hen and a cawing crow are a painful and unpleasant sound (*lupēron akousma kai aēdes*), but the imitator of hens and crows crying aloud delights. And when we see people withering, we are displeased, whereas we gladly look at the statues and paintings of people withering because our thought is led by the imitations in accordance with what is akin (674A11–674B8).

(iii) The Ambiguity of to hēdomenon

The Greek in Plutarch's passage becomes elusive at a critical juncture, particularly regarding the general statement attributed to the Cyrenaics. The term *to hēdomenon* is ambiguous. It can refer either to the subject experiencing pleasure (*what takes pleasure*, middle participle – Option B) or to pleasure as a subjective feeling (interestingly, equivalent to *to hēdesthai* – Option A).

We can dismiss a third possibility: that *to hēdomenon* means the (external) *pleasant thing* (i.e., as what causes pleasure). The word's range of meanings and the immediate context rule out that meaning altogether. It would be absurd that the Cyrenaics claim that pleasant (or painful) things are entirely unrelated to sight or hearing (*mē peri tēn opsin mēde peri tēn akoēn*).[108] On the contrary, sights and sounds also fall under what is pleasant and painful: Plutarch speaks of *painful sound* (*luperon akousma*), implying a causal relationship between external sounds and affective responses. He reinforces this through verbs or participles indicating causation – imitated bird sounds *delight* (*euphrainei*, 674B5; delightful sounds), the sight of suffering people *distress*es those who see them (*horōntes*, 674B5; distressing sights).

Turning to Option A, what would it mean to claim that pleasure in sights and sounds pertains entirely to thought, not perception? This remains vague unless we adopt Option B: *the subject of pleasure* is at stake. With a Platonist's dualism at play, aesthetic pleasures are *not* sensory pleasures – though involving perception – but pleasures the mind takes in. This aligns with *Quaes. Conv.* V's overarching framework, which distinguishes bodily from mental pleasures and argues for the primacy of the latter.[109]

This perspective is undeniably inappropriate for both Epicurean and Cyrenaic hedonism, making it astounding in addition that the Cyrenaics are reported to agree with the Platonist. Mapping Platonist dualism onto the hedonists' accounts does not do them justice. Epicureans register all pleasures in the soul. The question of whether their perceptual aesthetic pleasures belong to the mind is thus misguided, and denying it contradicts their view that the body neither perceives nor experiences pleasure. Instead, perception is a physiological process that involves the body and soul.[110]

Clearly, Plutarch does not frame this as a debate between cognitive and non-cognitive accounts of aesthetic pleasure in the Cyrenaic and Epicurean traditions but focuses on the bodily versus mental pleasure distinction. If he had intended such a contrast, he would not have acknowledged – at 673D – that the diners, among whom are some Epicureans, unanimously agree that it is the recognition of the actor's superiority to those genuinely afflicted by emotional suffering that accounts for the aesthetic pleasure. The reference suggests the Epicureans viewed aesthetic pleasure as involving propositional content. After all, he knows that Epicurus describes the sage as a *lover of spectacles*, taking the greatest pleasures in theatre, despite his critical stance on the arts (Plutarch *Non posse* 1095C; D.L. X.120).[111] This reduces the apparent contrast between the schools: both acknowledge cognitive aspects in aesthetic pleasure.

---

[108] Plutarch omits qualifiers like *merely* (*kata psilēn*, as in Diogenes Laertius' report).
[109] Plutarch allows *psychē* and *dianoia*, and their pleasures, to vacillate. In 672D (*peri tōn tēs psychēs kai sōmatos hēdonōn*), the genitive denotes both possession and the source of these pleasures.
[110] See D.L. X.63–6 (*Epist. Herod.*).
[111] On the nuanced Epicurean views on the arts, see Blank 2009.

Although Plutarch recognizes both commonalities (the cognitive aspect) and differences between the schools on this matter, he leaves much unsaid. The company of diners he portrays must have been familiar with these distinctions, but his presentation remains opaque. To maintain coherence in his argument and consider all the information he gives, we must accept that his primary concern – distorting though it is – is whether aesthetic pleasures belong to the body or the mind based on what causes them.[112]

(iv) Epicurean Aesthetic Pleasures Reconstructed

If we have read the Greek carefully and considered all textual evidence, the Cyrenaics would categorize aesthetic perceptual pleasures as pleasures of the mind according to Plutarch, and a paradox – if not a joke – emerges: the hedonists whom Epicureans criticize for focusing on present bodily pleasures may align more closely with Platonism than the Epicureans themselves. As said, however, Plutarch's arguments require caution, as he fails to do justice to either the Epicureans or Cyrenaics.

According to Epicurus, the specific experiences that Plutarch is acknowledging *in passing* in 637D should be analyzed into a pain due to the distressing sight or sound of the actor imitating a negative emotion and a pleasure caused by the belief that the actor is performing well. The sight or sound is painful and as such causes direct, unmediated perceptual pain in the theatre audience, that is, without the mediation of, and irrespective of, any thoughts entertained about the perceptual stimulus. The belief that the imitation is beautiful, appropriate, or skillful causes a distinct belief-based pleasure. Thus, the Epicureans account for the phenomenon of the 'same' perception (a genuine lament and a performance of a lament) eliciting opposite affective reactions by recognizing two distinct affective states in the audience. Giving up the unity of the aesthetic experience is the price they pay when reconstructing an aesthetic experience in the above way, unlike the single phenomenon the Cyrenaics register: a pleasant sound heard as a performance of lament, a single perceptual experience shaped not by a separate cognition.[113]

---

[112] Warren 2013 explains how the Epicurean analysis of aesthetic pleasures contrasts sharply with the Cyrenaic view, reflecting their distinct epistemologies. For Epicureans, the senses, and pleasures and pains, have criterial status, retained in simple perceptual pleasures unmediated by thought. While I refer to two affective states in Epicurean aesthetics, Warren rightly notes there may be more. He refines Plutarch's unclear text, defending the Epicurean account of aesthetic pleasures against the Platonist's usual charge of inconsistency. I cautiously – agreeing with Warren – assess the implications for the Cyrenaics in 674A–B. Unlike Warren, I find no clear textual support for a main focus on the debate about perceptual pleasure's cognitive or non-cognitive character between Cyrenaics and Epicureans, leaving Plutarch faring even worse than in Warren's version and misguiding the discussion.

[113] The Platonist framework permeates the text in a confusing manner, complicating efforts to establish reliable historical accounts of the hedonists. Consider 674C7–10, which

Moreover, a phenomenological objection could also challenge the Epicurean account. When the propositional content of an aesthetic experience changes (for example, the enjoyment of delightful singing in an opera, where one later discovers the lyrics convey an overtly sexist message in a language one initially did not understand), doesn't this transformation affect our perceptual affection? Does it not at least reduce the pleasure, if not entirely diminish it? Or, would we instead continue to experience a pleasant sound alongside an intellectual pain simultaneously, as separate and sequential reactions to our being informed about the meaning of the lyrics?

Unfortunately, Plutarch shows little concern for providing the necessary clarification. As we have demonstrated thus far, not only does he fail to do justice to the Epicurean view, but he also offers neither a consistent exposition of the subject nor even a clear articulation of the point of his critique. We have developed a critique of the Epicurean reconstruction and think that Plutarch raising the objection of the metaphysical unity of pleasure is the most coherent interpretation we can offer of the disputed testimony concerning the Cyrenaics (674A–B), seeking to reconcile it with the vague and ambiguous details Plutarch provides elsewhere in V.1 and to frame it as a robust philosophical critique aligned with, rather than contrary to, the spirit of the context.

(v) Conclusions and Implications

If this interpretation is correct, what can we infer about the Cyrenaics from this source? Should we trust Plutarch's report of Cyrenaic views? The Cyrenaics, after all, have not been otherwise shown to analyze aesthetic pleasures. Plutarch inserts them into a debate that interested him but likely did not concern them.[114] Aristippus focused on pleasure in general without distinguishing or prioritizing types, though bodily pleasures dominate the examples in surviving sources. Plutarch's claim that pleasures do not arise from sensation alone but from thought suggests that the true pleasant object (what really causes pleasure) is the thought, while the sensible object is only potentially pleasant or unpleasant, depending on how it is perceived. It does not do much justice to the Cyrenaics, just as Plutarch does little justice to the Epicureans with his overall framework.

Setting aside Plutarch's distorting agenda, the essential claim attributed to the Cyrenaics concerns experiences involving sights and sounds, which need not be aesthetic. In Diogenes' report, these are examples rather than the exclusive

---

acknowledges the same perceptual experience – the pig's sound (*to auto tēs aisthēseōs pathos*) – and differentiates the soul's affections (*oukh homoiōs diatithēsi tēn psuchēn*) with pleasure arising only when a particular thought is added (*hotan mē prosēi doxa* [...]). This formulation suggests a distinct judgment, mirroring the Epicurean view.

[114] Giannantoni 1958, 110, notes this is the only source where intellect plays a role.

focus. The common underlying structure remains: the Cyrenaics hold that we take in unified pleasures when perceiving things as pleasant, and pains when perceiving them as painful – an experience that is cognitively rich and does not chime that well with a Platonist dualism. Certainly, they do not accommodate the Epicurean raw or simple sense-perceptual pleasures (or pains).

Plutarch's use of *to hēdomenon* warrants examination in this context. The term is extremely rare in Greek literature. While neuter participles such as *to nosoun* and *to lupoun* appear in Sophocles and Thucydides (Soph. *Phil.* 674; Thuc. II.61.2), *to hēdomenon* is unattested before Plato. Its earliest occurrence is in his *Philebus*. Aristotle does not use it at all. It resurfaces in Epicurus, Diogenes of Oenoanda, and later Platonists, including Plutarch, who frequently uses neuter participles instead of abstract nouns (*to phoboumenon, to algoun, to ponoun, to tharroun*).[115] Damascius refines both grammar and metaphysics of pleasure in his *Philebus* commentary, *par.* 121, while Proclus, John Philoponus, and Simplicius also employ the term.

Since *to hēdomenon* originates in the *Philebus*, and given Plutarch's deep knowledge of Plato, his choice is likely deliberate. *Philebus* 37a1–38a4 forms part of an analysis (36c3–41a4) of falsehood in a specific category of pleasure – propositional pleasures, which are distinct from purely sensory or non-cognitive pleasures. Socrates draws a parallel between opining and taking pleasure (37a–b), dividing each into three elements: (a) the subject (*to doxazon* for opinion, *to hēdomenon* for pleasure); (b) the process (*to doxazein, to hēdesthai*); and (c) the object (*to doxazomenon* for opinion, *to hōi to hēdomenon hēdetai*, 37a9, for pleasure). This structure supports the possibility of false pleasure, paralleling the way opinions can be false, although the processes are always genuine.

If *to hēdomenon* originates in this context, what does this imply about Plutarch's report on the Cyrenaics? Given his familiarity with the *Philebus*, he likely employs a framework addressing hedonic error in propositional pleasure to reconstruct pleasure involving propositional content. This supports translating *to hēdomenon* as 'what takes pleasure'. However, it seems unlikely that Plutarch deliberately uses Cyrenaic terminology. In a passage where he does not provide precise quotations and alludes only loosely to Epicurean philosophy (as Teodorsson 1989, 139–46, notes about the proemium to *Quaes. Conv.* V), Plutarch's goal appears to be using the Cyrenaics as a tool to attack the Epicureans. Thus, it is unwise to assume this is a verbatim report of Cyrenaic claims or to take this passage as evidence that the Cyrenaics themselves engaged with *Philebus* distinctions.

---

[115] We find him using *to hēdomenon* in various other works: *Alex.* 22.7.1; *De Tuenda* 128C14; *Adolescens* 27C8; *De Adulatore.* 61B10; *De Iside* 380E3; *De Virt. Mor.* 447F3; *De Garr.* 513E9; *Non Posse* 1089E4; *De animae* 1025D11; *Maxime* 777C13.

Nevertheless, Plutarch intriguingly connects the Cyrenaic understanding of pleasure to a crucial passage from the *Philebus*. Aristippus likely did not adopt philosophical terminology from Platonic dialogues, yet he participated in and was influenced by relevant debates. Caution is necessary. Plutarch's report does not establish Aristippus as a mediator; it presumes this without direct evidence. The strongest support for this interpretation comes from Aristippus' own understanding of pleasure in Diogenes Laertius II.85.

2.3.3 Back to Aristippus: Applied Cognitivism

What might initially seem like mere anecdotal material of limited philosophical significance in Diogenes Laertius warrants closer examination. While it should not be mistaken for a systematic exposition of theoretical philosophical principles, it is a rich source for the Cyrenaic's character traits, behaviours, and reflections, which often resist reduction to specific themes such as pleasure. We will bring the section to a conclusion by arguing for the applicability of the structure of pleasure as elucidated through Diogenes' and Plutarch's sources in the anecdotes from the *Life* of Aristippus. This approach will allow us to opt for a continuity between Aristippus' and later Cyrenaic views on this subject. We will draw on certain reported events from his life, not with the aim of demonstrating theoretical presuppositions – adhering to the exposed principles of our investigation into Aristippus – but to show they can be plausibly reconstructed in a way that resonates with such an understanding of pleasure mediated by thoughts.

Put differently, our aim is not to attribute the cognitivist structure of pleasure to the father of the Cyrenaic School, but to show that the ancient material on him not only avoids contradicting it but also aligns with it. We will focus on three anecdotes that apart from those already drawn to shed light on the attitude on pleasure (Section 2.2.1) elucidate the cognitive elements underpinning the experience of pleasures according to the two reports we interpreted. These moments implicitly or explicitly involve affective states, both positive and negative, distressing and pleasant: at an incident at sea storm and the encounters with two rulers – Dionysius and Artaphernes – will serve as the basis for our analysis.

The fascination with philosophers' reactions during storms at sea has long been noted in storytelling. A well-known example is the Stoic philosopher who turned pale, as recounted by Aulus Gellius (*Attic Nights* XIX.1) or the placid Pyrrho (D.L. IX.68). Aristippus' response is attested in two sources, Diogenes Laertius II.71 and Aelian (*Varia Historia* IX.20), which complement one another. Not only does the report note his being alarmed and anxious, but also the cognitive content of his disturbance and anxiety: Aristippus is concerned about losing a happy life, whereas the other passengers risk only the loss of their miserable lives. This chimes well with the idea of pleasures and pains as cognitively rich. In this case, we have the same sensation (of the sea storm) and the same emotions of distress and anxiety that are caused due to the same thought that one is going to die. And yet, Aristippus adds the qualification that he is fearful that he will lose a happy life and, as a result, his distress and pain are different from his shipmates'. Though the story cannot help us pin down the structure of the generation of emotions, it powerfully highlights the role of cognitive content for the generation of the negative emotions at stake.

After being forced by the tyrant Dionysius to mention a philosophical doctrine, he replied that it was laughable that the tyrant learns from him the art of speaking and yet teaches him when he should talk. Having been punished by the offended tyrant and relegated to recline at the end of the table (usually the place of the least-honoured guest), Aristippus remarked that Dionysius merely sought to elevate the distinction of that place, which, though generally considered the least honourable, was now honoured by Aristippus' presence (*DL* II.73). A similar story, also centred on the fleeting significance of seating, is recounted in Athenaeus (Athen. XII. 544c–d), where the Cyrenaic ties the significance of the seat to his occupying it now. When encountering punishing words from the tyrant, the philosopher responds with a strikingly composed response. What emerges is not only a thought but an accompanying affective reaction, likely one of pleasure. Aristippus can avoid feeling distress by re-conceptualizing the situation; thinking of it differently changes how it feels. This aligns with the broader context, which emphasizes Aristippus' ability to transform varied circumstances into a source of pleasure.

Importantly, the same words could have elicited entirely different thoughts and, consequently, different and opposite emotions in another individual. Consider someone with low self-esteem or a tendency toward depression; such a person might interpret the tyrant's words through thoughts like, 'He does not see me as worthy', or might even activate a deeper negative core belief, such as, 'I am not worthy of respect'. These interpretations would likely give rise to negative emotions, such as pain and shame. This incident, along with our analysis, underscores the variability of cognitive appraisal in shaping emotional responses – specifically, the critical role of thought in the generation of emotions. Explicating the specific cognitive content in this incident further underscores a cognitivist approach to the generation of emotion.

When it was reported that Aristippus had been captured by Artaphernes, if that indeed occurred (D.L. II.79), and someone expressed surprise at his courage in the situation, Aristippus retorted that this was precisely the moment to be most courageous – just before having a conversation with the satrap. Clearly, there is cognitive content at play here as well, but the emotional state is complex and it remains unclear how to interpret the thought process that underlies his response. Courage does not exclude fear; on the contrary, it might require it. Although Aristippus seems to be driven by confidence and hope, both of which imply pleasure, it is not immediately clear why he would find hope and pleasure in speaking with the satrap. One possibility is that he simply enjoys conversing, which is attested in various sources; another could be that he harbours the hope of fascinating the satrap and persuading him to release him. Regardless of the reason, what is striking is that Aristippus transforms a situation that would be deeply distressing to most people into an opportunity for exercising courage, confidence, and hope, and the accompanying pleasure. The cognitive functions and elements involved become evident: he does not turn his attention to thoughts of potentially impending death, but to those that elicit pleasure, such as the act of conversing or conversing with the goal of securing his release.

These moments illustrate what it means for Aristippus to adapt to circumstances and turn any situation to his benefit (D.L. II.66). While he never formulated a formal theory of pleasure, and he did not analyse pleasures' structure as perceptions of things *as* pleasant, cognitive functions and elements were crucial in generating the pleasure he was able to experience in situations that might elicit the opposite emotion in others who accommodate different thoughts.

2.4 Philebus as a Present-Focused Hedonist

Hedonism takes many forms, with diverse types and variations. Even within a specific type, such as present-focused hedonism – which centres on present rather than past or future pleasures – significant differences emerge. For instance, some versions employ a hedonic calculus that prioritizes the present, as seen in later Cyrenaics' discussions with Epicurus or in the figure of Proximus in Parfit's *Reasons and Persons* (1984, 161 and passim). Others, such as Aristippan hedonism show no concern for maximizing pleasure or a calculus. Although both uphold the primacy of present pleasure, they need to be distinguished.

Further nuances exist even between hedonic presentisms that reject the calculus but still diverge on fundamental aspects – such as the presence or absence of concern for the quantity of pleasure and its priority, or the compatibility (or incompatibility) with a eudaemonistic concern about one's entire life. Versions of such hedonic presentisms may value reasoning and dialogue or, conversely, exhibit an aversion to such engagement. Consequently, we may ask whether their representatives agree more than they disagree.

Plato's dialogues present various types of hedonists, yet only one character, Philebus, qualifies as a representative of present-focused hedonism. Although a sporadic participant in the *Philebus*, he expresses a preference for present pleasure. This raises the question of whether Philebus exemplifies the same type of hedonism as Aristippus. Gosling and Taylor 1982, 166, acknowledge this possibility, stating that 'a case could also be made out for Aristippus being the target [...] one could easily suppose that Philebus is a stand-in for Aristippus'. However, they ultimately favour Eudoxus as the dialogue's primary interlocutor, citing the scarce sources on Aristippus and Cyrenaic philosophy, and the lack of Aristippus' presence in Aristotle's reports – whereas Eudoxan hedonism is explicitly discussed. They concede the circumstantial nature of their evidence about Eudoxus lurking at every turn in the dialogue (1982, 166), but still find Eudoxus the primary target.

I concur with their conclusion that Philebus is *not* a stand-in for Aristippus. However, I disagree with the methodological approach of identifying a singular 'main target' among Plato's contemporary hedonists in the dialogue.[116]

This section argues that Philebus' position differs fundamentally from Aristippan hedonism as reconstructed here. By juxtaposing these two forms of hedonism, we can further clarify the distinctive traits of the Aristippan model.[117]

2.4.1 The Character of Philebus

Platonic dialogues portray both those capable of engaging in dialectic and those who are not, revealing philosophy's rigorous prerequisites as Plato conceives it: a cooperative pursuit of truth that demands willingness to revise one's views rather than seeking personal advantage or status. The *Philebus* examines what state and disposition of the soul produce a good life (11d4–6), with pleasure and intellect as competing candidates, advocated by Philebus and Socrates respectively. The dialogue begins *in medias res*, after Philebus has abandoned the discussion. Though we lack details on the preceding exchange, Socrates summarizes the positions: Philebus maintains that pleasure and its kindred kinds constitute the good (11b4–c3),[118] a hedonistic thesis, as clarified at the

---

[116] See Section 2.4.3. Contra to Migliori 2000, 30–1, Gosling and Taylor were meticulous in formulating their thesis and never unreservedly interpreted Philebus as merely a 'mask for Eudoxus'.

[117] We compare Philebus and Aristippus not as individuals but as representatives of hedonistic types – *Philebus*, after all, is a fictional character.

[118] The sentence allows pleasure as one good among others, but 60a confirms Philebus' hedonistic claim that pleasure equals the good.

dialogue's end (60a). Moreover, Philebus presents pleasure as the proper aim for all living beings, attributing the function of final cause to pleasure while making both descriptive and normative claims about its role: all living beings naturally take pleasure to be good; therefore, pleasure is the highest good.[119]

However, mere assertion of a thesis does not meet Plato's conditions for dialectical engagement. A *logos* in Plato's sense is not just a statement but an account, explanation, and argument. To engage in *dialogos*, interlocutors must exchange reasons (*didonai kai dechesthai logon,* a dynamic which pragmatists Sellars 1954 and Brandom 1994 refer to in abbreviated form as 'the game of reasons'), rather than merely repeating claims, delivering monologues, or indulging in disconnected expositions. They must listen, identify agreements and disagreements, and advance together. Philebus likely abandoned the discussion because he merely reiterated his thesis without argumentation – perhaps citing the universal pursuit of pleasure as evidence. His disengagement after 28b6 suggests an aversion to dialectic itself, not just a fear of refutation, distinguishing him from figures like Callicles (*Gorg.* 505d–509c).

Philebus' retreat stems from his fundamental disregard for the reasoning which underpins dialogue. Socrates' summary of his thesis excludes reasoning (*logismos*) from among the goods, even as an instrumental good.[120] While Callicles might value debate for reputation, Philebus denies dialogue any function. His attitude is evident when, after Socrates establishes the main question – the ranking of lives of pleasure, intellect, or a mixture – Philebus simply asserts that pleasure wins in all cases (12a7–8), refusing to modify his stance. He tells Protarchus to decide for himself, isolating himself from the inquiry. Plato portrays Philebus as the polar opposite to the dialectical, philosophical nature.

Philebus' non-dialectical disposition is underscored when Socrates introduces the serious problems related to the unity and multiplicity of forms and the forms' relationship to individuals (15b1–c3). Protarchus suggests excluding Philebus, not out of hostility but due to their contrasting concerns:[121] Philebus indulges in physical pleasures while Socrates and Protarchus focus on metaphysical inquiry, pains, and pleasures (15d4–16b3). Protarchus mentions Philebus again when he is jestingly threatening Socrates that they will join in attacking him since he rails against young people who inappropriately exploit the metaphysics of unity and multiplicity (15d4–16b3), playfully invoking

---

[119] The argument relies on the universal pursuit of pleasure, central to Eudoxus' reasoning (Arist. *EN* X.2.1172b9–15). See Warren 2009 and Davies 2023.

[120] Thanks go to James Warren mentioning the instrumental value in the context and helping me detect an additional difference between Callicles and Philebus.

[121] Frede 1993, 7, playfully translates 15c9 that refers to Philebus as 'let sleeping dogs lie'.

Philebus' affinity with young men aligning with his name's etymology (*Philebos* = 'lover of youth').

Though Philebus remains somewhat attentive, his difficulty following Socrates is clear. When Socrates presents examples for the dialectical skill from grammar and music (16c5–17a5), Philebus asks why the argument concerns them and its purpose (18a1–2). Socrates welcomes these questions, as in Plato's dialogues, even the least dialectical interlocutors can contribute. In Plato's dialogues, every interlocutor – even Philebus – can serve as a voice through which Plato speaks. Both the aim of the argument and the reason it specifically engages these particular interlocutors are central to any example of Platonic dialectic. The argument does not unfold in abstraction but is addressed to particular interlocutors, taking into account their intellectual strengths and limitations to guide them toward the next step in the common pursuit of knowledge. It is a dialogue *with* them, not merely a display of argument for the sake of exposition; the latter is a practice that even sophists can perform.

Philebus presses the same question in 18d3–5, after Socrates has brought up the third example of dialectical skill: Theuth (18a6–d2). He understood more clearly the three examples of dialectical skill than the earlier abstract dialectical passage (18d3). All the same, Philebus continues, the current argument omits the same thing as those earlier one, namely, the question of how these arguments are relevant in the current inquiry into the ranking of lives.

Socrates responds that they have indeed encountered what they sought and explains the relevance to the topic discussed. Philebus follows the basics. However, Protarchus intervenes, actively building upon Socrates' remarks. Noticing that Philebus interferes, he reminds the group of the division of roles and reaffirms his commitment to be the successor and advocator of the Phileban thesis. Philebus, in turn, refrains from further interruption for now, deferring once again to the unfolding dialogue.

Philebus remains sporadically attentive, especially when his name is used, and reacts in 22c2–4 in a manner that reveals a combative concern rather than the spirit of a common pursuit of truth. To rebut Socrates' conclusion that Philebus' goddess, pleasure personified, is not to be identified with the good (22c1–2), he would need to argue against the preceding argument. Instead, he turns his attention to Socrates' alternative candidate, reason, to conclude a parity and underline the personal character of the debate: Socrates' candidate too cannot be identified with the good as the same charges stand for intellect as for pleasure.

He has a point, which shows that he followed the course of the argument, at least in broad strokes, though not in its fine nuances, for neither pleasure nor intellect should be identified with the human good.[122] The first prize is in fact allocated to the mixed life that combines both elements, and both the lives pleasure and intellect alone miss out. Then Socrates shifts from material causes (pleasure and intellect as elements of the mixed life) to the efficient cause of the good life: Which of the two, pleasure or intellect, makes a good human life good? To Socrates' challenge that pleasure will miss the second prize too, Protarchus, realizing that his candidate is in danger, intervenes again, and binds Socrates to his commitment to examine pleasure thoroughly.

It is noteworthy and relevant to our consideration of Philebus' capacity for Platonic dialectic, how Protarchus changes the tenor of the contest between pleasure and intellect. From a Philebean focus on the personal character of the debate, we turn to focus on pleasure as the topic of examination in 22e4–23a5. Protarchus personifies pleasure, and Socrates intellect. Though personified as combatants in the contest, the attention is rightly drawn back from Philebus and Protarchus, on the one hand, and Socrates, on the other, to the examination of the two combatants, with the interlocutors, Protarchus and Socrates united in this cooperative examination.

The remaining intervention from Philebus occurs after the second long and demanding digression into the fourfold ontology of limit, unlimited, mixture, and the (efficient) cause of mixture. Socrates addressed Philebus at a crucial point when analysing the third kind (the mixture of limit and unlimited) and acknowledged that Socrates' Aphrodite has deserted the hedonist's camp.[123] Socrates describes the goddess' role as imposing law and order on pleasures and their fulfillments, which have no limit in themselves, instead of representing pleasure without limit. He continues to address Philebus as someone who is afraid that pleasures and fulfillments are destroyed this way, whereas they are actually preserved by becoming moderate and orderly (28b5–c2), before turning to Protarchus again to resume the analysis of the fourfold division.

Socrates explains the connection to the central topic and the questions that they have raised so far (27c3–d3). Having established an agreement with Protarchus that the good and harmonious mixed life falls under the third kind of mixture, he turns to Philebus and asks a question about the Philebean life (*ho sos bios*, 27e1), that is, the life that comprises only pleasure and is unmixed with intellect or any cognitive elements. In fact, Socrates is keen on locating pleasure

---

[122] Had he been able to pursue the subtleties of the argument, he would have noted that a life of pleasure unmixed with any cognitive functions or elements is principally impossible for human beings.

[123] Philebus invokes Aphrodite as his witness, equating her with pleasure, but Socrates questions this (12b), explained in 26b–c. Pausanias distinguishes heavenly and earthly Aphrodite in *Symposium*.

as one of the contestants in their discussion (much more than arguing the nuances of the choice of lives at 20–2 with Philebus) and so offers Philebus a further hint:[124] Will pleasure accept the more and less, or does it involve limit? Philebus enthusiastically confirms that pleasure accepts 'what is more' and is the complete good exactly because it is unlimited in its nature regarding variety, quantity, and intensity. Socrates replies that given that pain also accepts 'what is more' and nonetheless is the complete evil, what makes pleasure good cannot be its being unlimited. Having taken the rejection personally, Philebus accuses Socrates of extolling his god, that is, intellect. Socrates ironically returns the compliment, and insists that they return to the question of where to classify understanding and intellect. Philebus requests that now Protarchus speak for him (28b6).

Philebus' final words in the dialogue mark the conclusion of his sporadic appearances, which serve primarily to reinforce his combative and uncooperative nature. He emerges as a character who takes philosophical inquiry personally, showing neither the capacity nor the inclination for a shared investigation into the nature and role of pleasure in the good human life. As a hedonist, he upholds pleasure as the highest good, reducing its evaluation to sheer quantity, with bodily pleasures – eating, drinking, and sex – being his sole concern. Though Philebus talks like a hedonist interested in devices that would secure as large a quantity of pleasure as possible, idleness seems to get in the way and we have no trace of the development of this idea. The only form of sharing that interests him is the shared enjoyment of those pleasures, not the exchange of ideas about their content or value. Needless to say, a personality so closed to discussion stands no chance of learning, let alone teaching. Throughout the discussion, he not only embodies this view but also displays an aversion to philosophy itself.

Philebus embodies the life of pure pleasure and nothing but pleasure, specifically, the pleasure he takes in at present. Though Socrates has rejected that life in 20–2 as a possibility for human beings, Philebus has not even noticed or followed the argument, nor is he ever asked about that content.[125] Instead, Socrates addresses him as someone living the life of unmixed pleasure as we saw above (as if that were possible).

A complete lack of cognitive faculties makes it impossible to judge that one is now experiencing pleasure, any recollection of past occasions of being pleased,

---

[124] Socrates shifts between life of *x* and concept *x*, as seen in the fourfold division and the third-kind-of-falsehood argument (43c8–44a11).

[125] See my analysis (Mouroutsou 2021) of the rejection of pure pleasure – unmixed with cognition – as an indirect proof (20–2), rejecting its possibility for humans, not its grade of goodness as less good than the mixed life.

or the anticipation and installation of future delight in the present moment. To be deprived of experiencing the past and future is detrimental to the amount of pleasure and, again, quantity is hedonists' concern. Eradicating memory and anticipation not only reduces the amount and intensity of pleasures but also threatens the existence of present pleasures. Plato's analysis of the anticipatory pleasures of bodily experiences, for instance, depicts present pleasure experiences as dependent on both the combination of past pleasures and pains, and the present calculation of future pleasures and pains (33 c–36 c). Experiencing even a single pleasure in the present is a complex matter, intricately dependent on cognitive faculties that enable our awareness of temporal unity and continuity.

Plato's *Philebus* presupposes a human life as a continuous whole that comprises past, present, and future. A human being is supposed to be pleased throughout a life (*dia biou*) when living a life of pleasure. Pleasure unmixed with intelligence, however, does not provide the grounds for a life because depriving humans of the cognitive activities that Socrates mentions reduces life to simple, successive moments of pleasure. The mere accumulation of moments – the paratactic existence of side-by-side hedonic episodes – does not produce, let alone bind together, a life. Therefore, the life of pleasure appears to collapse into the present moment of pleasure. But in addition, given the ignorance of one's state in this moment, one cannot even genuinely experience being pleased now.

Someone living a Phileban life, in that case, passively experiences time as a mere succession of present moments, each following the next without reflection or integration. To him, pleasure appears victorious now, just as it will seem victorious in the future – each 'future present moment' standing in isolation (cf. his paratactic formulation at 12a7: *I think* and *I will think*). This fragmented temporal experience, in which moments remain unconnected, underscores Philebus' exclusive preoccupation with the immediate present. The Socratic argument against the life of pleasure unmixed with intelligence, demonstrates that such a life, devoid of foresight or coherence, fails to constitute a human life at all.

2.4.2 Aristippus and Philebus

Though both Aristippus and Philebus are hedonists who centre their lives on the present moment, the vision of life we have reconstructed for Aristippus differs fundamentally from the one embodied by Philebus in Plato's dialogue.

(1) Aristippus demonstrates an inclination for dialogue, which he both valued and engaged in. Philebus, on the other hand, exhibits a deep aversion to argument and dialogue – an attitude that goes far beyond mere caution with

theoretical assumptions and language, which we have observed in Aristippus. If Aristippus had been akin to Philebus in this regard, his place among the Socratics would not only be perplexing but entirely ungrounded.

(2) In the extant fragments, Aristippus, as a hedonist, shows no concern for the quantity of pleasure. Maximization is not his objective, nor is there any indication that he engages in a hedonic calculus aimed at optimizing pleasure. On the contrary, we have situated his thinking within the euthymic model, as opposed to the maximizing model of well-being.

(3) Moreover, unlike Philebus, Aristippus does not advocate a life devoid of intelligence or cognitive elements. As reflected in the nuanced task of taking in pleasure 'as it comes', his approach entails discernment rather than passive indulgence. He does not simply surrender to whatever (exclusively bodily) pleasure presents itself; rather, he selectively attends to one among the many potentially pleasurable aspects of the present, recognizing its worth. Since the present always offers a variety of possible focal points, welcoming pleasure appropriately requires ongoing practice – an exercise in distinguishing which pleasures merit attention and in maintaining focus on one while disengaging from distractions. This also involves the ability to divert oneself from current pains, as far as the occasion allows it, and to resist dwelling on past or future suffering to the extent that it eclipses the present.

His conception of mastery over pleasure and the role of adopting the appropriate attitude in experiencing it further confirms that he does not advocate a life of nothing but pleasure. Instead of an exclusive or overt emphasis on bodily pleasures, Aristippus appears primarily concerned with cultivating the right disposition toward pleasure itself. Such intellectual gymnastics is totally alien to Philebus.

Furthermore, Aristippus does not reject the memory of past pleasure nor the anticipation of future pleasure, but takes them into consideration. There is no trace of such a view in the character of Philebus.

(4) Aristippus' lack of interest in the maximizing model does not imply indifference or opposition to a eudaimonistic vision that considers the whole of human life. Hedonistic eudaimonism is not bound to a single method – namely, hedonic calculation. As we have seen, Aristippus advances a distinct approach: a *policy* of living well, one that is therapeutic in nature, grounded in a euthymic model.

(5) Regarding the experience of time, while we cannot say much, we have reconstructed Aristippus' views as compatible with the notion of continuity of identity – since he recalls past pleasures and pains and anticipates future ones. On this account, he does not experience the present as an isolated moment disconnected from past and future, as Philebus does. Rather, he thinks of and

cares for past and future affections against the vision of progress he seeks in his attitude toward pleasures and pains.

2.4.3 A Final Note

The reason for considering Philebus here is that he is the only character in the Platonic corpus who unreflectively adheres to a presentist form of hedonism. However, this does not imply that Plato composed the *Philebus* as a direct response to Aristippus. There is no evidence to suggest that Plato regarded Aristippus' hedonism as significant enough to warrant a focused critique. More plausibly, Plato's work was motivated by the ideas of Eudoxus, a member of the Academy, whose formulation of hedonism Plato, like Aristotle, must have been deemed worthy of serious consideration.[126]

A deeper reason for Plato's approach lies in his portrayal of hedonism itself. When he depicts a hedonist, his interest lies in presenting a philosophical type. While doing that, he likely draws elements from different hedonistic approaches and theories. To assume, however, that he is mainly targeting a specific historical figure would reduce Plato to a mere historian rather than a philosopher.

One of the central achievements of *Philebus* is the culmination of Plato's twofold dialectical inquiry into pleasure, which exposes its metaphysical underpinnings through a critical dialogue with hedonists. Through this, Plato not only celebrates the rich discourse on the nature and role of pleasure within his Academy, but also advances a form of dialectic with hedonists that transcends its therapeutic function. In comparison to the psychotherapeutic engagement with specific individuals, such as Protagoras or Callicles, this dialectic is more depersonalized, though Socrates still examines both character and theses, as the case with Philebus shows. In this light, the notion that Plato's primary aim is to refute a particular hedonist appears inconsistent with the broader and multifaceted philosophical ambitions of the *Philebus*.

3 Beyond Historical Reconstruction: Aristippus and the 'Plasticity of the Present'

I now turn to a previously unexplored philosophical explanation of Aristippus' focus on the present: the 'plasticity of the present'.

We humans can focus on shorter or longer time intervals as present, usually adjusting automatically (i.e., without reflection) depending on the context and our state. For instance, when obliged to orchestrate multiple tasks under considerable stress, we focus on the immediate present instead of thinking about the

---

[126] This plausible assumption is shared by Gosling 1975, 139–41, Karpp 1933, 23–7 and Giannantoni 1958, 145–54.

year ahead – for example, while composing an urgent email – typically without reflecting on the fact that we need to do so or that we are doing so. When in distress, we intentionally redirect our attention to the immediate task, allowing all others to fade, albeit not always successfully, which might exacerbate our distress. This is not true for those experiencing major clinical depression or even its remission, who struggle to choose the appropriate range of temporal attention, and do not automatically or deliberately correct themselves and narrow down the adaptive scope after initially failing. They cannot discern when they should restrict or expand their temporal attention.[127]

Because of this possibility of extension and restriction, we can say that the present moment is 'plastic'. Marcus Aurelius in his *Meditations* explains how it is up to the agent to retrench or expand the present time, depending on their state of mind and moral progress.[128] When succumbing to emotions of fear and distress, for instance, Marcus Aurelius advises himself to divert his attention from considering his whole life and restrict it to a shorter present time or, if possible, to the very specific current task. On the other hand, he also exploits the possibility of expanding his present time to encompass his entire life, when in the first book he expresses his thanks to all the people who have shaped his character up to that point. The Stoic sage's present could be so 'expanded' as to encompass the entire cosmic time between the conflagrations, with the past being the time of the past universe before the last conflagration and the future the time of the subsequent emerging world.[129]

This plasticity has important benefits and uses for psychological well-being. Indeed, it can be added as a new subcategory of attention-deployment for modern emotion regulation theory and psychotherapy. Additionally, we can envisage an educational approach for treating depression through this practice in constructive dialogue with models in cognitive behavioural therapy and interventions for depression pioneered by Watkins 2016 and Dalgleish 2023; Hitchcock et al. 2017 and 2018.[130]

---

[127] This builds on material in Mouroutsou (in press). The general account of shifting attention from the general to the specific levels of action and goal identification and vice versa according to the various contexts has been experimentally shown with regard to the general and specific levels and is being currently reconsidered: Watkins 2011.

[128] Aur. VII.36 emphasizes narrowing thinking to the immediate present; Aur. XII.3 focuses on present life for the sage; Aur. I, by one not a sage, thanks all who shaped him throughout his present life.

[129] See Mouroutsou 2020 which compares Marcus Aurelius' view on time in harmony with Chrysippus' on time and the present by using the notion of 'retrenchability', mainly developed by Schofield 1988, and also shows the additional influence of the Epictetan distinction between what is up to us and what is not up to us on Aurelius' thought about time.

[130] As developed in Mouroutsou (in press).

The framework of the 'plasticity of the present' can be formulated as follows in contemporary discussions about ethics: In certain contexts, it is reasonable or rational (psychologists might add: adaptive) to delimit the present more narrowly than in other contexts, in which it is reasonable or rational to engage with a more 'expanded' present. Thus, the rationality or reasonability of restricting or expanding the present time is context-dependent.

We might restrict the present, for instance, if we are overburdened by too many tasks. Other such contexts involve receiving bad news about a failure, being in an unfamiliar environment in life or a *terra incognita* that emerges in a research project, or experiencing intense emotional distress. In such cases, it is rational to narrow one's focus to a more immediate present than to dwell on a longer duration. Otherwise, one risks exacerbating distress, in this way impeding present and future well-being, and making non-optimal decisions.

We might expand the present in periods characterized by greater security, inner peace, and external stability. In such contexts, it becomes reasonable or useful to raise broader questions like those about one's traits and behaviours to understand and perhaps also change them – for example: 'Why do I tend to respond in a certain way in specific situations?' Addressing such questions involves focusing on more extended periods, identifying patterns in particular episodes, drawing general conclusions about character and types of behaviour, and formulating goals and habituation plans should one wish to change their behaviour. One might also decide on long-term matters, such as retirement planning. Attempting to make such decisions while plagued by inner distress or external instability would be both unreasonable and irrational.

The way I have formulated the 'plasticity of the present' does not answer the principal question that shapes much of the debate about time neutrality and time relativity, for it is not concerned with attaching or denying intrinsic significance to the present time as part of a human life considered as a whole, beside past and future time. It does not address the present as a time in which benefits or harms are located within the agent's life and is not concerned with whether it should be privileged among other time locations as increasing the good(s) and the bad(s) intrinsically, all other factors being equal.[131]

Because 'the plasticity of the present' neither affects the value of different parts of a whole (past, present, and future being the parts of an entire human life

---

[131] The formulation of the prevalent ethical question can be found in various authors involved in the debate about time neutrality and time relativity ever since Sidgwick 1907, 381, defined the principle of neutrality as an 'impartial concern for all parts of our conscious life', adding that 'the mere difference of priority and posteriority in time is not a reasonable ground for having more regard to the consciousness of one moment than to that of another'. Among others, consider Slote 1983, 9–37; Brink 2003, 215; Brink 2011; Williams 1995.

in this case) nor the relationships between those parts and life as a whole, the relevant prudence at stake differs, too. The prudence of an agent does not depend on whether they are equally concerned with all parts of their life (i.e., time neutrality) or assign greater value to the past, present, or future (i.e., time relativity). Rather, the agent's expansion or restriction of what they count as the present is shaped by both internal and external factors – such as inner peace or overwhelming anxiety, cognitive schemas and vulnerability (internal states), and conditions of stability or insecurity in one's family, friendships, or work environment (external contexts).

Nevertheless 'the plasticity of the present' is certainly crucially related to time (though not time location in the above respect) and considerations about well-being both in one's present moment and one's entire life. Plasticity in this sense is not a quality that belongs to the present time in itself but rather refers to the agents' capacity to locate themselves in time by delineating the specific present they should focus on in the relevant context. Therefore, 'the plasticity of the present' shapes a new question that is both meaningful in itself and helpful for ethical discussions that take psychology into account.

Let us return to and reread the third part of Text B, Gel. *VH* XIV.6, which has been found influenced by later Stoic thought according to our earlier results about Marcus Aurelius' plasticity of the present moment, and reread it:

> He prescribed that people keep their thought *on the day, and again on that part within the day in which each one takes some action or thinks*; for only the present is ours, he said, not what has gone by or what is anticipated, for the one is lost, and the other is uncertain if indeed it will be. Gel. *VH* XIV.6.

Although this report does not expand the present to consider one's life as a whole, it supports the plasticity of the present in one's present day: one might focus on the entire present day or a shorter part of the day relevant to one's action or thought – that is, one delineates the present adaptively. Both ancient sources on Aristippus' focal concern with the present attribute a lack of epistemic clarity to future times,[132] which is particularly helpful to consider alongside the concept of the retrenchable present. What we delineate when we choose the temporal frame to which it is adaptive to refer and attend as 'present', may be the present day or the present meal or the present paper – but we can expand from the day to the year and even to one's entire life. And this is precisely where we draw the boundaries of epistemic clarity and obscurity: the greater the epistemic unclarity, the more we narrow down the present.

---

[132] Compare in Athenaeus that past 'is no longer' and future 'is not yet and is uncertain' (again the word is *adēlon*).

Drawing the right boundaries shapes our capacity to make sound decisions about action, offer refined reflection, and foster understanding of our lives as developing wholes in which the present is not prefixed as a part of a mathematical whole, but is constantly being determined by us in the given circumstances.

By marking divergences between historical contexts and contemporary philosophical presuppositions, ancient texts can be approached with historical precision and philosophical self-reflection.[133] This fosters both faithful historical reconstruction and a dialogue that is mutually illuminating for the history of philosophy and contemporary philosophy, opening new interpretive possibilities relevant to both ancient and modern contexts. In this way, the history of philosophy, specifically, ancient philosophy, proves philosophically significant beyond its own domain.[134] The hypothesis of the plasticity of the present and the resulting euthymic model of well-being – developed thanks to ancient philosophy, including the ethical outlook of Aristippus, and in critical dialogue with the maximizing model of rationality – may also inform contemporary discussions in philosophy and psychotherapy to be pursued elsewhere.

---

[133] I adopt Michael Frede's approach to, and evaluation of, the 'historical history of philosophy' (2022, 9–18), adding that we cannot conduct it fully free of our philosophical presuppositions.

[134] For a remarkable resonance between such an approach to the history of ancient philosophy, on the one hand, and to ancient and contemporary philosophy, on the other, and Chang's integrated practice of history and philosophy of science, see Chang 2011.

Abbreviations

My abbreviations for classical authors follow those of *LJS* and the *Oxford Latin Dictionary* (ed. P.G.W. Clare, 1982, Oxford, Clarendon Press). When not registered by either, I follow the *Oxford Classical Dictionary* (eds. S. Hornblower, A. Spawforth, and E. Eidinow, 2012, Oxford, Oxford University Press). I provide them here for quick reference. All translations are my own. The citations to Plato and Aristotle follow Stephanus ed. 1578 and Bekker ed. 1831 respectively. In the following list, I use the translations of book titles in the Loeb Classical Library series (Harvard University Press).

ANCIENT AUTHORS AND WORKS

Ael. = Aelian; *VH* = *Varia Historia* (*Historical Miscellany*)

Aesch. = Aeshylus; *Pers.* = *Persians*

Arc. = Arcadius; *De Acc.* = *De Accentibus* (*On Accents*)

Arist. = Aristotle; *EN* = *Ethica Nicomachea* (*Nicomachean Ethics*); *Met.* = *Metaphysics*; *Rh.* = *Rhetoric*

Athen. = Athenaeus, *Deipnosophistae* (*The Learned Banqueters*)

Aur. = Marcus Aurelius, *M. Antonius Imperator Ad Se Ipsum (Meditations)*

Cic. = Cicero; *Fin.* = *De Finibus* (*On Ends*); *Tusc.* = *Tusculanae Disputationes* (*Tusculan Disputations*)

Clem. Al. = Clemens Alexandrinus; *Paedag.* = *Paedagogus* (*The Paedagogue*); *Strom.* = *Stromata* (*Miscellanies*)

Cyril. *in Jo. Ev.* = *Cyrillus Alexandrinus, Commentary of the Gospel of John*

Dem. = Demosthenes; Dem. 56 = Demosthenes, *Against Dionysodorus*

D.L. = Diogenes Laertius, *Lives of the Philosophers*

Epict. = Epictetus; *diss.* = *dissertationes* (*Discourses*); *Ench.* = *Encheiridion* (*Manual*, compiled by Arrian)

Epicurus. *Ep. Men.* = *Epistula ad Menoeceum* (*Letter to Menoeceus*); *Sent. Vat.* = *Sententiae Vaticanae* (*Vatican Sayings*)

Eur. = Euripides; *Ba.* = *Bacchae*; *Hec.* = *Hecuba*

Eus. *PE* = Eusebius of Caesarea, *Praeparatio Evangelica* (*Preparation for the Gospel*)

List of Abbreviations

Gel. *Noct. Att.* = Aulus Gellius, *Noctes Atticae* (*Attic Nights*)

Gnom. Vat. = *Gnomologium Vaticanum* (an anonymous Byzantine anthology of philosophical sayings preserved in a Vatican manuscript)

Hdt. = Herodotus *Histories*

Longin. *Proll. Heph.* = Longinus (the grammarian), *Prolegomena ad Hephaestionem* (*Prolegomena to Hephaestion*)

Luc. *Vit. Auct.* = Lucian, *Vitarum Auctio* (*The Sale of Lives*)

Matthew = New Testament, *Matthew*

Maxim. Tyr. *Phil.* = Maximus of Tyre, *Philosophical Orations*.

Phld. = Philodemus; *De elect.* = *De Electionis et Fugis* (*On Choices and Avoidances*)

Plat. = Plato; *Gorg.* = *Gorgias*; *Phaedo* = *Phaedo*; *Phileb.* = *Philebus*; *Prot.* = *Protagoras*; *Tim.* = *Timaeus*

Plut. = Plutarch; *Adolescens* = *Quomodo adolescens poetas audire debeat* (*How the Young Man Should Study Poetry); Alex.* = *Alexander*; De Adulatore = *De adulatore et amico (How to Tell a Flatterer from a Friend); De Animae* = *De animae procreatione in Timaeo* (*On the Generation of the Soul in the Timaeus); De Cur.* = *De curiositate* (*On Being a Busybody*); *De Garr.* = *De garrulitate* (*Concerning Talkativeness); De Iside* = *De Iside et Osiride;* De Tuenda = *De tuenda sanitate praecepta* (*Advice about Keeping Well*); *De Virt. Mor.* = *De Virtute Morali* (*On Moral Virtue)*; *Maxime* = *Maxime cum principibus philosopho esse diserendum* (*That a Philosopher Ought to Converse Especially with Rulers); Quaes. Conv.* = *Quaestiones Convivales* (*Table-Talk*); *Non Posse* = *Non posse suaviter vivi secundum Epicurum* (*That Epicurus Actually Makes a Pleasant Life Impossible*)

[Plut.] *Strom.* = Pseudo-Plutarch, *Stromata* (*Miscellanies*); [Plut.] *Vit. Hom.* = Pseudo-Plutarch, *De Vita Homeri* (*On the Life of Homer*)

Sch. D. T. = *Scholia in Dionysii Thracis Artem Grammaticam* (*Commentaries on Dionysius Thrax' Art of Grammar*)

S. E. = Sextus Empiricus; *M* = *Adversus Mathematicos* (*Against the Dogmatists*), which encompasses *Against the Professors*, *Against the Logicians*, *Against the Physicists* and *Against the Ethicists*.

Sen. = Seneca; *Brev. Vit.* = *De Brevitatae Vitae* (*On the Shortness of Life*); *Ep.* = *Epistulae Morales* (*Epistles*)

Soph. = Sophocles; *Phil.* = *Philoctetes*

Stob. *Ecl.* = Stobaeus, *Eclogae* (*Selections*)

Them. *Or.* = Themistius, *Orationes* (*Orations*)

Thuc. = Thucydides, *Historiae*

Xen. = Xenophon; *Mem.* = *Memorabilia*

MODERN WORKS

Diels, H. (1879) Diels, H. (1879^1, 1979^5) *Doxographi Graeci*, Berlin, De Gruyter (= *Dox. Graec.*).

Diels, H. (1903^1; 1956^6). *Die Fragmente der Vorsokratiker: Griechisch und Deutsch*, W. Kranz (ed.), Berlin, Weidmann. (= *DK*) Berlin, Weidmann. (= DK).

SSR = Giannantoni, G. (1990) ed. *Socratis et Socraticorum Reliquiae*, Vols. I–IV, Naples, Bibliopolis. (= *SSR*).

LJS = Liddell, H. G. and R. Scott. (1996) *A Greek-English Lexicon*. Revised and augmented throughout by Sir Henry Stuart Jones, with the assistance of Roderick McKenzie, and with the cooperation of many scholars, Oxford, Clarendon Press.

SVF = von Arnim, H. ed. (2004; 1902^1) *Stoicorum Veterum Fragmenta*. Vols I-IV, München and Leipzig, K. G. Saur Verlag. (= *SSR*).

References

Allen, J. (2014) 'Why There Are Ends of Goods and Evils in Ancient Ethical Theory' in M. Lee (ed.), *Strategies of Argument. Essays in Ancient Ethics: Epistemology, and Logic*, Oxford, Oxford University Press, pp. 231–254.

Annas, J. (1993) *Morality of Happiness*, Oxford, Oxford University Press.

Bett, R. (2005) *Sextus Empiricus: Against the Logicians*, Cambridge University Press, Cambridge.

Blank, D. (2009) 'Philosophia and Technē: Epicureans on the Arts' in J. Warren (ed.), *The Cambridge Companion to Epicureanism*, Cambridge, Cambridge University Press, pp. 216–233.

Brandom, R. (1994) *Making it Explicit: Reasoning, Representing, and Discursive Commitment*. Cambridge MA, Harvard University Press.

Brink, D. O. (2003) 'Prudence and Authenticity', *Philosophical Review*, 112, pp. 215–245.

Brink, D. O. (2011). 'Prospects for Temporal Neutrality' in C. Callender (ed.), *The Oxford Handbook of Philosophy of Time*, Oxford, Oxford University Press, pp. 353–381.

Bury, R. G. transl. (1935). Sextus Empiricus, Against the Logicians, Cambridge MA, Harvard University Press.

Chang, H. (2011) 'Beyond Case-Studies: History as Philosophy' in S. Mauskopf and T. Schmaltz (eds.), *Integrating History and Philosophy of Science*, Boston Studies in the Philosophy of Science, 263, pp. 109–124.

Chiesara, M. L. (2001) *Aristocles of Messene: Testimonies and Fragments*, Oxford, Oxford University Press.

Dalgleish, T. and H. Caitlin (2023) 'Transdiagnostic Distortions in Autobiographical Memory Recollection', *Nature Reviews Psychology*, 2, pp. 166–182.

Davies, R. (2023) *The Hedonism of Eudoxus of Cnidus*, Cambridge, Cambridge University Press.

Diels, H. (1879^1, 1979^5) *Doxographi Graeci*, Berlin, De Gruyter (= *Dox. Graec.*).

Diels, H. (1903^1; 1956^6). *Die Fragmente der Vorsokratiker: Griechisch und Deutsch*, W. Kranz (ed.), Berlin, Weidmann. (= *DK*).

Dodds, E. R. (1960) ed. and comm., *Euripides: Bacchae*, Oxford, Oxford University Press.

Dorandi, T. (2013) ed. *Diogenes Laertius: Lives of Eminent Philosophers*, Cambridge, Cambridge University Press.

Döring, K. (1988) *Der Sokratesschuler Aristipp und die Kyrenaiker*, Mainz, Akademie der Wissenschaften und der Literatur.

Dozois, D. and A. Beck (2008) 'Cognitive Schemas, Beliefs and Assumptions' in K. S. Dobson, and D. J. A. Dozois (eds.), *Risk Factors in Depression*, Oxford, Elsevier/Academic Press, pp. 121–143.

Feldman, F. (2004) *Pleasure and the Good Life*, Oxford, Oxford University Press.

Fuchs, T. (2018) 'The Cyclical Time of the Body and its Relation to Linear Time', *Journal of Consciousness Studies*, 25, pp. 47–65.

Frede, D. trans. and introd. (1993) *The* Philebus, Cambridge MA, Hackett Edition.

Frede, M. (2022) *The Historiography of Philosophy*, K. Ierodiakonou (ed.), Oxford, Oxford University Press.

Furley, W. (1992) 'Antiphon der Athener. Ein Sophist als Psychotherapeuter?' *Rheinisches Museum fuer Philologie*, 135, pp. 198–216.

Giannantoni, G. (1958) *I Cirenaici, raccolta delle fonti antiche: Traduzione e studio introduttivo*. Naples, Bibliopolis.

Giannantoni, G. (1990) ed. *Socratis et Socraticorum Reliquiae*, Vols. I–IV, Naples, Bibliopolis. (= *SSR).*

Goldhill, S. (2009) 'The Anecdote: Exploring the Boundaries Between Oral and Literate Performance in the Second Sophistic' in W. A. Johnson and H. N. Parker (eds.), *Ancient Literacies: The Culture of Literacy in Greece and Rome*, Oxford, Oxford University Press, pp. 96–113.

Gosling, J. C. B (1975) ed. and comm. *Plato: Philebus*, Cambridge, Cambridge University Press.

Gosling, J. C. B. and C. C. W. Taylor (1982) *The Greeks on Pleasure*, Oxford, Clarendon Press.

Graver, M. (2002) 'Managing Mental Pain: Epicurus vs. Aristippus on the Pre-rehearsal of Future Ills', *Proceedings of the Boston Area Colloquium in Ancient Philosophy*, 17, pp. 155–177.

Gulick, C. B., trans. (1933). Athenaeus of Naucratis: *The Deipnosophists*. Volume V, Books 11–12, Cambridge MA, Harvard University Press.

Hitchcock, C., A. Werner-Seidler, S. Blackwell, and T. Dalgleish (2017) 'Autobiographical Episodic Memory-Based Training for the Treatment of Mood, Anxiety and Stress-Related Disorders: A Systematic Review and Meta-Analysis', *Clinical Psychology Review*, 52, pp. 92–107.

Hitchcock, C., S. Gormley, C. Rees, E. Rodrigues, J. Gillard, I. Panesar, I. M. Wright, E. Hammond, P. Watson, A. Werner-Seidler, and T. Dalgleish (2018) 'A Randomised Controlled Trial of Memory Flexibility Training (MemFlex) to Enhance Memory Flexibility and Reduce Depressive

Symptomatology in Individuals with Major Depressive Disorder', *Behaviour Research and Therapy*, 110, pp. 22–30.

Indelli, G. and V. Tsouna-McKirahan (1995) *Philodemus: On Choices and Avoidances*, Naples, Bibliopolis.

Irwin, T. (1991) 'Aristippus Against Happiness', *The Monist*, 74, pp. 55–82.

Karrp, H. (1933) *Untersuchungen zur Philosophie des Eudoxus von Knidos*, Würzburg-Aumühle, Triltsch.

Kazantzis, N., F. M. Datillio, K. S. Dobson and J. Beck (2017) *The Therapeutic Relationship in Cognitive-Behavioral Therapy: A Clinician's Guide*, New York, Guilford Publications.

Kechagia, E. (2011) 'Philosophy in Plutarch's Table Talk: In Jest or in Earnest?' in F. Klotz and K. Oikonomopoulou (eds.), *The Philosopher's Banquet: Plutarch's Table Talk in the Intellectual Culture of the Roman Empire*, Oxford, Oxford University Press, pp. 77–104.

Kindstrand, J. F. (1986) 'Diogenes Laertius and the Chreia Tradition', *Elenchos*, 7, pp. 219–243.

Lampe, K. (2015) *The Birth of Hedonism*, Princeton, Princeton University Press.

Long, A. A. (1999) 'The Socratic Legacy' in K. Algra, J. Barnes, J. Mansfelt and M. Schofield (eds.), *The Cambridge History of Hellenistic Philosophy*, Cambridge, Cambridge University Press, pp. 617–641.

Mann, W. R. (1996) 'The Life of Aristippus', *Archiv für Geschichte der Philosophie*, 78, pp. 97–119.

Mannebach, E. (1961) *Aristippi et Cyrenaicorum Fragmenta*, Leiden, Brill.

Migliori, M. (2000) *Filebo* (tr. It., intro., and comm.), Milan, Bompiani.

Mill, J. S. (2018) *Autobiography*, M. Philp (ed.), Oxford, Oxford University Press.

Mouroutsou, G. (2020) 'The Plasticity of the Present Moment in Marcus Aurelius' Meditations', *Ancient Philosophy*, 40, pp. 411–434.

Mouroutsou, G. (2021) 'Choosing a Life and Rejecting a Thoughtless Life in *Philebus* 20–22', *Ancient Philosophy*, 41, pp. 393–412.

Mouroutsou, G. (2024) 'Therapeutic Presentisms: A Hedonist and a Stoic in Agreement?', *History of Philosophy and Logical Analysis*, 26, pp. 321–340.

Mouroutsou, G. (in press) 'The Plasticity of Temporal Attention: Training a Healthier Mind as Inspired by Marcus Aurelius' in T. Fuchs, *The Phenomenology of Emotion Regulation: Feeling and Agency*, Oxford, Oxford University Press.

O'Keefe, T. (2002) 'The Cyrenaics on Pleasure, Happiness, and Future-Concern', *Phronesis*, 47, pp. 395–416.

O'Reilly, K. (2019) 'Cicero Reading the Cyrenaics on the Anticipation of Future Harms', *Epoché*, 23, pp. 431–443.

Parfit, D. (1987) *Reasons and Persons*, Oxford, Clarendon Press.

Rohland, R. A. (2023) *Carpe Diem: The Poetics of Presence in Greek and Latin Literature*, Cambridge, Cambridge University Press.

Rowe, C. (2015) 'The First-Generation Socratics and the Socratic Schools: The Case of the Cyrenaics' in U. Zilioli (ed.), *From the Socratics to the Socratic Schools: Classical Ethics, Metaphysics and Epistemology*, London, Routledge.

Rudolph, F. (1894) 'Zu den Quellen des Aelian und Athenaios', *Philologus*, 52, pp. 652–663.

Schofield, M. (1988) 'The Retrenchable Present' in J. Barnes and M. Mignucci (eds.), *Matter and Metaphysics: The Fourth Symposium Hellenisticum*, Bibliopolis, Naples, pp. 329–374.

Sedley, D. (2017) 'Epicurean vs. Cyrenaic Happiness' in R. Seaforth, J. Wilkins and M. Wright (eds.), *Selfhood and the Soul: Essays on Ancient Thought and Literature in Honour of Christopher Gill*, Oxford, Oxford University Press, pp. 89–109.

Segal, Z. V., M. G. J. Williams and J. D. Teasdale (2013) *Mindfulness-Based Cognitive Therapy of Depression*, New York, Guilford Press.

Sellars, W. (1954) 'Some Reflections on Language Games', *Philosophy of Science*, 21, pp. 204–228.

Sidgwick, H. (1907) *Methods of Ethics* (1874^1, 1907^7), Cambridge MA, Hackett Edition.

Slote, M. (1983) *Goods and Virtues*, Oxford, Oxford University Press.

Slote, M. (1989) *Beyond Optimizing: A Study of Rational Choice*, Cambridge MA, Harvard University Press.

Sommerstein, A. E., ed. and trans. (2009) Aeschylus. *Persians. Seven Against Thebes. Suppliants. Prometheus Bound*, Cambridge MA, Harvard University Press.

Strawson, G. (2004) 'Against Narrativity', *Ratio*, 17, pp. 428–452.

Tarán, L. (1981) *Speusippus of Athens: A Critical Study with a Collection of the Related Texts and Commentary*, Leiden, Brill.

Tarrant, H. (1994) 'The Hippias Major and Socratic Theories of Pleasure' in P. Vander Waerdt (ed.), *The Socratic Movement*, Ithaca New York, Cornell University Press, pp. 107–126.

Teodorsson, S. T. (1989) *A Commentary on Plutarch's Table Talks*, Vols I–II, Göteborg, Acta Universitatis Gothoburgensis.

Trapp, M. B. (1994) *Maximvs Tyrivs Dissertationes*, Stuttgart and Leipzig, Teubner.

Tsouna-McKirahan, V. (1994) 'The Socratic Origins of the Cynics and the Cyrenaics' in P. Vander Waerdt (ed.), *The Socratic Movement*, Ithaca New York, Cornell University Press, pp. 367–391.

Tsouna, V. (1998) *The Epistemology of the Cyrenaic School*, Cambridge, Cambridge University Press.

Tsouna, V. (2002) 'Is There an Exception to Greek Eudaemonism?' in M. Canto-Sperber and P. Pellegrin (eds.), *Le Style de la Pensée: Recueil de Textes en Hommage à Jacques Brunschwig*, Paris, Les Belles Lettres, pp. 464–489.

Tsouna, V. (2016) 'Cyrenaics and Epicureans on Pleasure and the Good Life: The Original Debate and its Later Revivals' in S. Weisser and N. Thaler (eds.), *Strategies of Polemics in Greek and Roman Philosophy*, Leiden, Brill, pp. 113–149.

Tsouna, V. (2020) 'Aristippus' in D. C. Wolfsdorf (ed.) *Early Greek Ethics*, Oxford, Oxford University Press, pp. 380–411.

Urstad, K. (2018) 'Aristippus on Freedom, Autonomy and Pleasurable Life' in A. Stavru and C. Moore (eds.), *Socrates and the Socratic Dialogue*, Leiden and Boston, Brill, pp. 179–201.

von Arnim, H. ed. (2004; 1902^1) *Stoicorum Veterum Fragmenta*. Vols I-IV, München and Leipzig, K. G. Saur Verlag. (= SVF).

Warren, J. (2001) 'Epicurus and the Pleasures of the Future', *Oxford Studies in Ancient Philosophy*, 21, pp. 135–179.

Warren, J. (2009) 'Aristotle on Speusippus on Eudoxus on Pleasure' in *Oxford Studies in Ancient Philosophy*, 36, pp. 249–281.

Warren, J. (2013) 'Epicureans and Cyrenaics on Pleasure as a Pathos' in S. Marchand and F. Verde (eds.), *Épicurisme et Scepticisme*, Roma, Università la Sapienza, pp. 127–144.

Warren, J. (2014a) *The Pleasures of Reason in Plato, Aristotle and the Hellenistic Hedonists*, Cambridge, Cambridge University Press.

Warren, J. (2014b) 'Cyrenaics' in J. Warren and F. C. C. Sheffield (eds.), *The Routledge Companion to Ancient Philosophy*, London, Routledge, pp. 409–422.

Watkins, E. R. (2011) 'Dysregulation in Level of Goal and Action Identification Across Psychological Disorders', *Clinical Psychology Review*, 31, pp. 260–278.

Watkins, E. R. (2016) *Rumination-Focused Cognitive-Behavioral Therapy for Depression*, New York and London: Guilford Press.

Williams, B. (1995) 'The Point of View of the Universe: Sidgwick and the Ambitions of Ethics' in B. Williams, *Making Sense of Humanity: And Other Philosophical Papers 1982–1993*, Cambridge, Cambridge University Press, pp. 153–171.

Acknowledgements

This study developed from a larger project, *Plato's Twofold Dialectic of Pleasure: Critical Dialogue with Hedonists and Critical Analysis of Pleasure*. What began as an extended digression grew into a self-standing inquiry.

I am indebted to the audiences whose feedback guided me as I developed the project in its initial stages: the 45th Annual Ancient Philosophy Workshop, the Classical Association Conference 2023, and the Eastern Division of the American Philosophical Association 2024. I especially thank Christopher Moore for his thoughtful comments at the APA, and Verity Harte, Mary Margaret McCabe, and David Sedley for stimulating discussions.

James Warren deserves special gratitude for his sustained and engaging dialogue and his remarkable speed in offering invaluable assistance. I am equally grateful to Tim O'Keefe for his thorough and profoundly helpful report and to Nicholas Denyer for insightful comments and discussions. I am particularly grateful to Tim Dalgleish and Edward Watkins for conversations which, as part of my interdisciplinary exchange with clinical psychology, revealed unexpected ways in which this field can inform ancient philosophical research.

I gratefully acknowledge the support of the Social Sciences and Humanities Research Council.

Cambridge Elements

Ancient Philosophy

James Warren
University of Cambridge

James Warren is Professor of Ancient Philosophy at the University of Cambridge. He is the author of *Epicurus and Democritean Ethics* (Cambridge, 2002), *Facing Death: Epicurus and his Critics* (2004), *Presocratics* (2007) and *The Pleasures of Reason in Plato, Aristotle and the Hellenistic Hedonists* (Cambridge, 2014). He is also the editor of *The Cambridge Companion to Epicurus* (Cambridge, 2009), and joint editor of *Authors and Authorities in Ancient Philosophy* (Cambridge, 2018).

About the Series
The Elements in Ancient Philosophy series deals with a wide variety of topics and texts in ancient Greek and Roman philosophy, written by leading scholars in the field. Taking a theme, question, or type of argument, some Elements explore it across antiquity and beyond. Others look in detail at an ancient author, a specific work, or a part of a longer work, considering its structure, content, and significance, or explore more directly ancient perspectives on modern philosophical questions.

Cambridge Elements

Ancient Philosophy

Elements in the Series

Plato's Ion: Poetry, Expertise, and Inspiration
Franco V. Trivigno

Aristotle on Ontological Priority in the Categories
Ana Laura Edelhoff

The Method of Hypothesis and the Nature of Soul in Plato's Phaedo
John Palmer

Aristotle on Women: Physiology, Psychology, and Politics
Sophia M. Connell

The Hedonism of Eudoxus of Cnidus
Richard Davies

Properties in Ancient Metaphysics
Anna Marmodoro

Vice in Ancient Philosophy: Plato and Aristotle on Moral Ignorance and Corruption of Character
Karen Margrethe Nielsen

Stoic Eros
Simon Shogry

Suspension of Belief
Daniel Vazquez

Contemplation and Civic Happiness in Plato and Aristotle
Dominic Scott

Plato's Unwritten Doctrines
Carl Séan O'Brien

Aristippus of Cyrene, Pleasure and the Present
Georgia Mouroutsou

A full series listing is available at: www.cambridge.org/EIAP

For EU product safety concerns, contact us at Calle de José Abascal, 56–1º,
28003 Madrid, Spain or eugpsr@cambridge.org.

www.ingramcontent.com/pod-product-compliance
Lightning Source LLC
LaVergne TN
LVHW011855060526
838200LV00054B/4345